THE
EVERYTHING®
Rock Drums Book

Dear Reader,

Writing *The Everything® Rock Drums Book* has been a joy for me and I hope that you find my advice and musical examples to be both helpful and inspirational. This book should serve as a starting point for your own research. Unfortunately, I can't tell you literally everything there is to know about rock drumming; there is simply not enough room in any publication for that. But even if I could, that would spoil the fun. Part of learning is trial and error and self-exploration: stress the "self."

Use this book as a resource, as a guiding hand, and as a point of departure. Every attempt has been made to create a thoughtful, well-balanced, and comprehensive text. However, much more information can be gleaned through careful investigation. See Appendix A and B for some tips on where to begin. In the end, it all comes down to practicing, listening, and performing. If you do this on a regular basis, you *will* get better. Along the way, seek expert advice from respected local musicians in your area and, if possible, celebrity drummers.

My very best to you, and good luck!

Eric Alan

Welcome to the EVERYTHING® Series!

These handy, accessible books give you all you need to tackle a difficult project, gain a new hobby, comprehend a fascinating topic, prepare for an exam, or even brush up on something you learned back in school but have since forgotten.

You can choose to read an *Everything*® book from cover to cover or just pick out the information you want from our four useful boxes: e-questions, e-facts, e-alerts, and e-ssentials. We give you everything you need to know on the subject, but throw in a lot of fun stuff along the way, too.

We now have more than 400 *Everything*® books in print, spanning such wide-ranging categories as weddings, pregnancy, cooking, music instruction, foreign language, crafts, pets, New Age, and so much more. When you're done reading them all, you can finally say you know *Everything*®!

QUESTIONS?
Answers to common questions

FACTS
Important snippets of information

ALERTS!
Urgent warnings

ESSENTIALS
Quick handy tips

PUBLISHER Karen Cooper

DIRECTOR OF ACQUISITIONS AND INNOVATION Paula Munier

MANAGING EDITOR, EVERYTHING SERIES Lisa Laing

COPY CHIEF Casey Ebert

ACQUISITIONS EDITOR Lisa Laing

DEVELOPMENT EDITOR Brett Palana-Shanahan

EDITORIAL ASSISTANT Hillary Thompson

Visit the entire Everything® series at *www.everything.com*

THE EVERYTHING® ROCK DRUMS BOOK

WITH CD

From basic rock beats and syncopation to fills
and drum solos—all you need to perform like a pro

Eric Starr

Adamsmedia
Avon, Massachusetts

Dedicated to Joe Morello: an innovator and a mentor to many.

An Everything® Series Book.
Everything® and everything.com® are registered trademarks of F+W Media, Inc.

Published by Adams Media, a division of F+W Media, Inc.
57 Littlefield Street, Avon, MA 02322 U.S.A.
www.adamsmedia.com

ISBN 10: 1-59869-627-0
ISBN 13: 978-1-59869-627-1

Printed in the United States of America.

J   I   H   G   F   E   D   C   B   A

Library of Congress Cataloging-in-Publication Data
available from the publisher.

*This book is available at quantity discounts for bulk purchases.
For information, please call 1-800-289-0963.*

Contents

1960s Innovators 161

Hard Rock and Heavy Metal 175

Neil Peart and Drum Composition 189

Progressive Rock 203

Stewart Copeland and Rock Hybrids 217

Jazz-Rock and a New Breed of Drummers 231

Concepts for Success 245

Equipment Guide 255

Appendix A:
Essential Recordings, Books, and Films/DVDs 264

Appendix B: Websites 267

Index 269

Acknowledgments

Thanks to Lisa Laing and the entire staff at Adams Media, Inc. Also, thanks to Marc Schonbrun for his "cogent" technical advice. Furthermore, thanks to Katherine Starr and Jeffrey Starr for the photos. Special thanks to Nelson Starr for engineering, producing, and mastering the audio CD. All performances by Eric Starr.

Top Ten Things You'll Learn from This Book

1. How to read and interpret drum notation.

2. How to play a wide variety of rock beats (also called grooves).

3. How to play a wide variety of drum fills orchestrated around a five-piece drum kit.

4. How to solo in a meaningful, logical fashion. You will learn about structure, call and response, using repetition, and much more.

5. How to play various subgenres of rock including funk, hard rock, progressive rock, heavy metal, jazz-rock, and much more.

6. You will learn about the history and evolution of rock music from the 1940s to the present.

7. You will learn about key innovators on the drum set including Ringo Starr, Keith Moon, John Bonham, Neil Peart, Bill Bruford, Stewart Copeland, Vinnie Colaiuta, and many others.

8. Tips for practicing, which will maximize your efficiency and rate of progress.

9. How to purchase the right gear to meet your needs.

10. Tips for further study. A comprehensive list of recordings, books, DVDs, and websites is provided for you in the back of this book.

Introduction

▶ Welcome to *The Everything® Rock Drums Book*! This publication will not only teach you how to play rock drums, it will show you how to be a better musician. Will you actually learn everything about rock drumming? No book can literally teach you *everything* there is to know about any topic. This book does, however, detail the salient points of playing rock. In other words, it outlines the key elements of rock drumming and it gives you the information you need to make wise musical decisions. Ultimately, this book is designed to enlighten, inspire, and empower.

The body of *The Everything® Rock Drums Book* is structured in three distinct parts. This system excludes Chapter 1, which is a brief historical primer. The first major section—Chapters 2–11—is cumulative and sequential: It's a series of interconnected building blocks that move from basic note reading to more advanced rock grooves, fills, and solos. The goal with this section is to teach you how to read music, how to develop stick control, how to play various beats, how to orchestrate fills around the kit, and how to solo in a logical and meaningful manner.

The first section of this book mentions specific drummers, but the second part—Chapters 12–17—is centered on the innovators themselves. In this section, you will analyze real players, learn a little bit about their backgrounds, and gain insight into each drummer's legacy. Where possible, this book has tried to avoid overloading you with reams of biographical material since, in most cases, this can be found online with relative ease. Therefore, each chapter in section two focuses on drummer X's sound and style. Where possible, musical examples support the text. These examples are not literal transcriptions; they are notational outlines used to illuminate the underlying musical idea behind each beat, fill, or solo.

The third section of the book deals with musical concepts, tips, and resources. This ranges from maintaining a positive attitude to playing in a band to choosing the right drum set for you. Lastly, two appendices are provided. One focuses on essential recordings, books, and DVDs; the other is a comprehensive list of websites about drums and drumming.

Overall, *The Everything® Rock Drums Book* moves through beginner material rather quickly. So if you're brand new to drumming, you should first learn from a basic snare drum manual; there are many on the market to choose from. This book jumps into *real* rock drumming rather quickly, and this requires you to have some prior experience with the instrument.

The accompanying disc features many of the original beats, fills, and solos found in this book. However, due to the space limitations, each beat is played only twice and each fill is played only once. Also, only select beats and fills are played from most figures. The examples performed on the CD are listed underneath the music. On the CD, the tempo of each pattern is moderate, except when the music is intended to be fast. Tempo indications should be viewed as goals, not commandments.

When playing the notated examples, you will see repeat symbols used. Where multiple examples are grouped together in a list (e.g. 1–8), the repeat symbol is used *only* at the end of the example. In an actual piece of music, a start repeat would be written at the beginning of the section to show you where to repeat back to. In a real musical context, if one is not indicated, you should assume that the repeat takes you back to the beginning of the song. However, in this book, you should *not* assume this! The repeat symbols simply mean to go back and repeat the beginning of the *specific exercise* you are practicing; this is usually a one-measure beat or fill.

When reading drum set notation, be sure to read it *vertically*, or up and down. If you don't, your beats will not be aligned properly. Here's how it works: Instruments that play together are lined up vertically in the notation. For example, if you see a hi-hat note on beat one and a bass drum note *directly under it* on beat one, you should assume that these instruments are played simultaneously. The same would be true of a snare drum note that is vertically aligned with a cymbal or a tom-tom, etc. Attention to detail is crucial here. If you don't understand how to play something, listen to the CD. If it is not performed on the disc, or you still don't understand it, study the corresponding text. If you're still confused, find a qualified instructor to coach you.

Chapter 1

History of Rock Music

Before you play rock, or any kind of music, it's important to gain a historical perspective. Rock, like any other style, has both forerunners and offspring. In this chapter, you will learn about the rich and diverse history of rock. You'll also get a sense of where rock may be headed in the future. Bear in mind that this chapter cannot possibly introduce you to every aspect, movement, artist, or subgenre of rock. Use the following information as a springboard for your own research.

In the Beginning: The 1950s

After World War II, big band and swing music began to decline as a new form of music took shape. This new style borrowed from rhythm and blues (R&B) and the fiery electric blues of Chicago and Detroit. It also embraced a variety of folk and country music styles from Texas, Appalachia, and the Deep South.

When rock 'n' roll emerged in the early 1950s, it altered popular music forever. The term was first used in the tune "My Baby Rocks Me With One Steady Roll" (1922) by blues singer Trixie Smith. However, it was Alan "Moondog" Freed who first used the phrase "rock 'n' roll" on his Cleveland radio show in 1951. The 1951 Sun Records release "Rocket 88," penned by a young Ike Turner, is viewed by many as the first rock 'n' roll release. Rock 'n' roll gained popularity in large part due to the sales boom of electric guitars, jukeboxes, televisions, and 45 RPM records that coincided with America's post-War prosperity. Key figures such as Freed, Sam Phillips, Jack Clement, Jerry Leiber, Mike Stoller, and others all took advantage of this technology by drawing white audiences and musicians alike to participate in the birth of a new era.

Although many proto rock 'n' roll musicians were black, rock's first superstar was Elvis Presley, a white singer from Tupelo, Mississippi. Presley added a spirited backbeat to traditional country music, along with a strong dose of R&B, to create a sound that was completely fresh and original to popular audiences. The result was a subgenre of rock 'n' roll called rockabilly. Along with Presley, Sam Phillips's recording facility, Sun Studio, and his independent label, Sun Records, would produce some of the key players in the nascent rock n' roll movement, including Jerry Lee Lewis, Carl Perkins, Johnny Cash, and Roy Orbison.

FACT

Located at 706 Union Avenue in Memphis, Tennessee, Sun Studio was originally called the Memphis Recording Service. Many rock 'n' roll and country pioneers recorded at Sun, including Elvis Presley, Carl Perkins, Johnny Cash, Jerry Lee Lewis, and Roy Orbison. In the late 1980s, the Irish band U2 also recorded at the Union Avenue location.

While early rock 'n' roll borrowed from many styles, it would ultimately develop unique musical and social characteristics. For example, rock 'n' roll rebelled against the establishment in ways no other style of music had done before. In fact, rock was openly defiant, much to the chagrin of 1950s suburbanites who grew up on Glenn Miller and Bing Crosby. Unlike their swing-music predecessors, rock 'n' roll musicians wore radical clothing and embraced drastic hairstyles. Soon, pompadours, greased ducktails, leather jackets, and denim pants became symbols of rock's bold attitude.

Musically speaking, rock 'n' roll used a heavier backbeat than earlier styles of music. (As you will learn, rock drum grooves typically employ bass drum patterns on beats one and three and snare drum patterns on beats two and four.) Rock 'n' roll also relied on amplification to get a larger-than-life sound. Structurally, rock songs were hook-laden and they avoided AABA song forms used by songwriters of the Great American Songbook. Lastly, rockers often engaged in suggestive dancing and other stage theatrics when performing. All this served to heighten the experience of the music.

Rock 'n' roll made its unofficial crossover to white audiences when Elvis Presley recorded "That's Alright Mama" in 1954. However, it was his 1956 number-one hit, "Heartbreak Hotel," that cemented rock 'n' roll's influence on popular culture. Artists such as Chuck Berry, Fats Domino, Buddy Holly, Bill Haley, Little Richard, and others also contributed significantly to rock 'n' roll's popularity during the 1950s. Arguably, the three most important rock drummers from this era are Elvis's drummer, D. J. Fontana, Buddy Holly's drummer, Jerry Allison, and session drummer Earl Palmer, who is noted for his work with Fats Domino and Little Richard.

Rock Emerges: The 1960s

In the 1960s, rock would drop its "roll" and mature into a whole range of substyles. Artists such as Jimi Hendrix, The Who, The Rolling Stones, Bob Dylan, Janis Joplin, The Doors, and The Beatles were on the forefront of this emerging music.

In 1964, with the arrival of The Beatles on American shores, rock music took on a new, arguably deeper, meaning in popular culture. No other band has influenced the course of modern musical history more than "The Fab Four." To this day, The Beatles remain the most significant rock/pop group of our time. In truth, they have become something of a musical institution.

FACT

The Beatles were active from 1960–1970. Band members included John Lennon, Paul McCartney, George Harrison, and Ringo Starr. Former members included Stuart Sutcliffe (bass) and Pete Best (drums). The Beatles hailed from a city in Northwest England called Liverpool. They are the originators of the "Merseybeat" sound. In the late 1960s, they were also pioneers of "psychedelic rock."

In the early 1960s, The Beatles borrowed from 1950s rock 'n' roll. They were very influenced by Chuck Berry, Eddie Cochran, Carl Perkins, Little Richard, The Everly Brothers, and Elvis Presley. However, they soon developed a unique sound, quickly copied by their contemporaries. Moreover, their songwriting genius can be heard as early as 1963 on the album *With the Beatles*.

In their later period, The Beatles found inspiration in the music of Bob Dylan and The Beach Boys' seminal album *Pet Sounds*. However, it was The Beatles who were ultimately defining the sound of their generation. Today, The Beatles continue to influence—both directly and indirectly—the music of many genres, and it's unlikely that their influence will ever cease. Albums such as *Revolver, Sgt Pepper's Lonely Hearts Club Band, The White Album*, and *Abbey Road* were among the most important albums of the 1960s, if not the latter half of the twentieth century.

Despite this, the "British Invasion" was not limited to The Beatles. The Kinks, The Yardbirds, The Who, and The Rolling Stones were some of the English bands that swept the United States and Canada in the mid-1960s. This musical cavalcade would embrace 1950s rock 'n' roll and blues, but with an eagerness to experiment and combine styles at will. For example, The Rolling Stones drew heavily from bluesman Muddy Waters. However, they were also influenced by Eastern music, as evidenced by the song "Paint it Black" from the record *Aftermath* (1966).

The United States also produced some legendary rock musicians in the 1960s. For example, Jimi Hendrix revolutionized rock with his blues-influenced guitar pyrotechnics. The renegade folkie, Bob Dylan, became one of the first singers to bring deep, poetic meaning to a decade of turbulence and civil unrest. When he "went electric," recording and touring with a backing group in the mid-'60s, his music crossed over into rock.

> The Woodstock Music and Art Fair (August 1969) was a pivotal event in rock. Promoted as "Three Days of Peace and Music," Woodstock was the gathering place of some of rock's finest artists, including Carlos Santana, Janis Joplin, The Grateful Dead, Creedence Clearwater Revival, The Who, The Band, Jimi Hendrix, and many others. Nearly 500,000 people attended the festival.

West Coast artists The Doors and Janis Joplin also had an impact on rock in the 1960s. The Doors were a mercurial, yet arty, group that featured Jim Morrison's poetic lyrics and Ray Manzarek's pulsating Vox Continental organ. The jazzy drumming of John Densmore and the guitar leads of Robby Krieger completed this band's wholly unique vibe.

Janis Joplin was another important trailblazer in this decade. Joplin was one of the first female rock singers to be recognized during the 1960s. Joplin's brand of raspy blues singing changed listeners' perceptions of women in rock. Her vocal style stood in stark contrast to dulcet folk artists Joan Baez, Joni Mitchell, and Judy Collins. Unfortunately, Joplin's life was cut short in 1970—at the age of twenty-seven—due to a drug overdose. The Doors' front man, Jim Morrison, also died at age twenty-seven due to a self-destructive lifestyle. Additionally, Hendrix's life was cut short due to a lethal combination of alcohol and sleeping pills. Like Joplin and Morrison, he was also only twenty-seven.

Progressive Rock

Almost since the beginning, rock has mutated into several offshoots or sub-genres. In the 1970s, these substyles became more clearly defined. While "soft rock" ruled the Top 40 airwaves in the '70s, other ambitious styles of rock were developing. One of these styles was "progressive rock."

Progressive rock, or "prog-rock," was first played in the late 1960s. However, it became especially popular in the early to mid-1970s. By the end of the '60s, select bands—mostly from England—began experimenting with long, complex song forms. These groups typically mixed classical and jazz with rock, creating novel stylistic hybrids. Eventually, the music of Emerson, Lake & Palmer (ELP), Genesis, Pink Floyd, King Crimson, Yes, The Soft Machine, and Jethro Tull became known as "progressive." Sometimes, these groups were also called "art rock" bands.

None of these groups concentrated on three-minute pop tunes. Nor did they follow any sort of pop structural formula. In other words, they did not construct songs solely around verses, choruses, and bridges; such devices were often seen as limiting or restrictive. In many cases, these elements were disregarded altogether.

E ALERT!

Prog-rock, by its very nature, allows for a variety of personal styles. Therefore, no two prog-rock bands are alike. For example, Pink Floyd's ethereal, and often moody, albums are very different from the buoyant, classically inspired work of Emerson, Lake & Palmer. In general, the open-ended, experimental nature of prog-rock promotes individualism.

Many prog-rock groups presented their songs like miniature symphonies. Their music often contained themes and variations, recapitulations, and grandiose musical detours. Often, this meant extended instrumental interludes, unexpected tempo shifts, odd time-signatures, surprising key changes, and exotic modal explorations. All of this required a technical virtuosity that many earlier rockers did not possess. Also, just about any style of music was fodder for prog-rock musical experimentations. Various styles of classical, jazz, blues, folk, world, and even country and western found their way into prog-rock "anthems."

Despite the many creative elements of prog-rock, this subgenre remains one of the most criticized styles of rock music. Some listeners have called prog-rock excessive, extravagant, and even pompous (perhaps with good reason). However, fans of the music enjoy the almost cinematic experience of listening to "prog songs."

Hard Rock and Heavy Metal

Hard rock and heavy metal both emerged in the 1970s. "Hard rock" is a pat term used to describe bands that have a hard-edged, powerful sound. It is the opposite of soft rock, which is generally more radio friendly, streamlined, and pop oriented. Hard rock is based on heavy-hitting drums, distorted guitars, and intense vocals. Improvisation—usually flashy guitar solos—is also a hallmark of hard rock.

Hard rock can be difficult to distinguish from heavy metal, its stylistic offshoot. Just remember that heavy metal is an extreme, over-the-top version of hard rock. Moreover, heavy metal is less blues based. In metal, guitarists generally favor pentatonics over bluesy scales. (A blues scale uses flatted thirds, fifths, and sevenths; pentatonics are consonant, five-note scales.) Because of this, metal guitarists are often referred to as "shredders."

Heavy metal also favors power chords, which are nonspecific chords that do not contain thirds. On the other hand, hard rock employs chordal variety in addition to power chords. Furthermore, heavy metal bands often rely on hyper-fast speeds or very heavy, loping grooves. Hard rock is always "cutting," but by comparison, it is less extreme and more diverse.

Rush is a Canadian "progressive hard rock" band that remains very popular to this day. A power trio consisting of Geddy Lee on bass and vocals, Alex Lifeson on guitar, and Neil Peart on drums, Rush has released over twenty albums since 1974. Rush offers the instrumental virtuosity fans have come to expect in prog-rock and the fire and intensity listeners crave in hard rock.

While powerful in nature, hard rock still tends to fall back on blues riffs, and it's not uncommon to hear dynamic (loud and soft) shifts in the music. This might include mellow sections or psychedelic, spacey elements followed by explosive playing. The music of Led Zeppelin is one example of this. Further, hard rock usually offers a melodic hook in the chorus of each song. While heavy metal *also* favors hooks, they may be less obvious to listeners, especially in later periods where the music blooms into all-out "speed metal" and "thrash metal."

Some important hard rock bands are Led Zeppelin, Deep Purple, Rush, Van Halen, Aerosmith, Guns N' Roses, Soundgarden, and Alice in Chains. But be careful of labels in music. Guns N' Roses has also been branded "sleaze glam" and Soundgarden and Alice in Chains, along with Nirvana and Pearl Jam, are also pioneers of "grunge rock." Grunge is a regional sub-set of a bigger, wide-open style of rock called "alternative rock."

Other bands that walk the line between hard rock and heavy metal include AC/DC and KISS. Straight-up metal bands include the early British innovators Judas Priest, Black Sabbath, Iron Maiden, and Motorhead. Additional metal bands—popular in the mid-to-late 1980s—include Mötley Crüe, Def Leppard, Dokken, Pantera, Ratt, Quiet Riot, Slayer, Megadeth, and Metallica. Keep in mind that metal bands do not all play the exact same style(s). For example, Mötley Crüe, Def Leppard, and Ratt played "glam metal" or "hair metal." On the other hand, classic Metallica is best described as "thrash metal." One thread that weaves through all heavy metal is the size of the drum set. Double bass drums, large power tom-toms, and vast arrays of cymbals are universal features on heavy-metal kits.

Punk and New Wave

Punk music flourished in the late 1970s and early '80s, but ultimately it would be replaced by another style of music called "new wave." In the early '80s, new wave was promoted as a friendlier version of punk rock. Punk was hard to market on the radio, since it was a raw, sometimes vulgar, form of garage rock.

Punk thrived best in the underground music scenes of London and New York where disgruntled youths used it to denounce conservative values and bleak futures. The Ramones, a New York band, were one the first punk innovators. In England, punk railed against the establishment and Margaret Thatcher. The Sex Pistols' "Anarchy in the UK" is the best example of this. In this song, singer Johnny Rotten calls himself an "antichrist." He also yells, "Get Pissed Destroy." New York-based punk singer Patti Smith was a key innovator in the United States. Unlike the Sex Pistols, she brought incisive poetry and scathing intellectualism to punk.

New wave is really nothing more than a catch phrase used to describe a variety of pop groups and solo artists that gained popularity in the late '70s and early '80s. The music created by these groups was not always similar, but it coincided with the advent of MTV and the emerging digital age. Some of these artists also had punk roots, but they ultimately favored pop hooks and radio singles even if leftist political views remained fervent. Such was the case with The Clash, who might be termed "punk-pop" *and* new wave.

FACT

Most new-wave artists were from the UK. However, America and Australia also churned out successful new-wave bands. One of the most influential new-wave groups was The Cars from Boston, Massachusetts. Blondie and Devo were also important American new wavers. Australia produced Men at Work, who topped the charts with "Who Can it Be Now" and "Down Under" in 1982.

New wave coincided with major advancements in synthesizer technology, and many new-wave bands used these instruments to achieve a slick musical polish. Use of drum machines and electronic drum pads were also popular during the early 1980s. The hexagonal Simmons pads were extremely popular electric drums. Also, digital drum machines were used to augment, and sometimes replace, acoustic drums. The Linn LM-1 was the first to use digital (as opposed to analog) samples. Artists such as Gary Numan, The Human League, and Peter Gabriel were among the first to experiment with Linn technology.

Key new-wave bands/artists include Tears for Fears (UK), Duran Duran (UK), Joe Jackson (UK), Elvis Costello (UK), Eurythmics (UK), The Cure

(UK), Peter Gabriel (UK), Depeche Mode (UK), Blondie (USA), The Cars (USA), The Talking Heads (USA), and Devo (USA). Some of these groups also fit under the "synth-pop" category. Perhaps the most iconic of all new-wave groups was The Police (1977–1986), a group that blended elements of new wave, punk, and reggae. You will more learn about this inimitable band, and their drummer Stewart Copeland, in Chapter 16.

New wave reached its peak in 1985 with Live Aid, a massive concert for Ethiopian hunger relief. Singer Bob Geldof, of the Boomtown Rats, organized this hugely successful concert, which featured a cornucopia of new-wave and other rock artists.

Rock in the 1990s and Beyond

The 1990s are best defined by "alternative rock." Alternative rock began in the 1980s, but the term wasn't widespread in its use until around 1990. Of all the labels used to catalog rock, alternative rock may be the broadest. Initially, alternative rock was used to describe the music of bands that were not signed to the Big Six record labels, which were Warner Brothers, Sony, PolyGram, BMG, Universal, and EMI. (BMG and PolyGram have now merged with Sony and Universal respectively.) In other words, alternative rock was a term applied to independent or "indie rock" artists. However, the term has now been stretched to embrace major-label bands that mimic the underground, garage, or street feel of indie bands. Because of this, the tag "alternative rock" is something of a misnomer in today's market. In fact, alternative is now very much the mainstream.

In the early 1990s, however, alternative rock had at least a tincture of purity. And in the American Northwest, alt-rock produced a substyle called "grunge." Initially, grunge was released on Sub Pop Records, an independent record label from Seattle, Washington. However, soon the major labels harnessed the power of grunge with *Nevermind* by Nirvana and *Ten* by Pearl Jam. These albums captured the ears of Generation X listeners throughout the United States and eventually the world.

Grunge was a stripped-down, back-to-basics style of rock. Gone were the fancy synthesizers and electronic drums of the 1980s. Gone were the showy guitar licks and, for the most part, the operatic vocal gimmicks of heavy metal. Also, drum kits were slimmed back to four-piece setups and novelty cymbals and double kick drums were discarded along with Flying V guitars and teased-up hair.

Grunge draws its power from hard rock, heavy metal, and punk. Bands such as Nirvana, Pearl Jam, Alice in Chains, and Soundgarden created music with a heavy punch, and today their musical ethos still resonates with alternative rockers. Despite this, the grunge movement was not long lived. It gradually fell out of fashion after Nirvana's singer, Kurt Cobain, died in 1994.

It is difficult to make projections about rock's future. However, it's clear that technology will play a major role in the twenty-first century. Home recording tools, playback (listening) devices, instrument manufacturing, and purchasing options will have a dramatic effect on *all* music. Due to advances in computer, digital, and cellular technology, consumerism is changing rapidly too. Without a doubt, rock is already feeling this impact in both positive and negative ways. But one thing's for sure: rock will continue to evolve as the twenty-first century unfolds.

Chapter 2

Reading Music

In this chapter, you will review standard notation. If you're brand new to notation, it's recommended that you first learn the elementary musical examples from Chapter 4 of *The Everything® Drums Book* or work your way through a beginner snare drum method. This chapter is intended only to be a brief tutorial. Nonetheless, if you're fuzzy about basic notational concepts, this is the place to start. This book uses notation extensively, so you will want to make sure that your music-reading skills are up to par.

The Importance of Reading Music

Reading music is very important. You should learn how to read music for the same reasons you learn how to read words. If you're musically literate, your chances of survival in the world of music greatly improve. Musical notation is also an important educational tool. Through notation, you will be able to visualize drum parts better and be able to conceive of music more lucidly.

This is not to say that playing by ear is wrong or bad. In fact, ear playing should be encouraged. Ignorant musicians have long pitted "readers" against "ear players," as if there is a conflict between reading music and feeling music. However, smart musicians will tell you that *both* reading and listening skills are important.

Listening cannot be underestimated, and all musicians should learn how to pick up a tune by ear. However, playing only by ear is limiting, especially when you are trying to learn information from a book. The CD in the back of this guide is a great supplement, but it cannot replace the notation found in each chapter. Therefore, in order to get the most out of this text, make sure you learn how to read music.

Understanding Notes

All music can be divided into two parts: sound and silence. Notes represent the sounds a musician makes; rests indicate silence. Both are written on a staff, a set of five parallel lines on which a composer writes notes, rests, and other musical symbols. Figure 2-1 shows you a blank staff.

FIGURE 2-1:
A blank staff

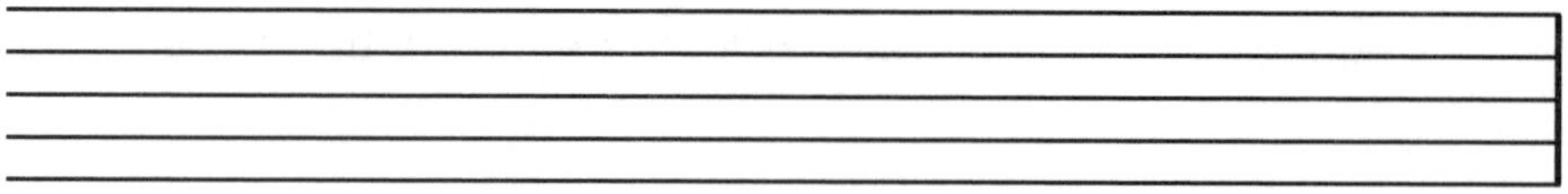

The lines and spaces on a staff represent pitch varieties, and a clef is used to name each line and space. The most common clefs are treble, or G, clef and bass, or F, clef. However, since most drums are indefinite pitched instruments, you will use a neutral clef and follow an instrument legend. For example, look at the spaces on the staff in Figure 2-1. On a drum set, the bottom space is used for the bass drum. One space above this is used for the floor tom-tom. The next space up is used for the snare drum, and the top space is used for the first rack tom-tom (usually a 10"- or 12"-diameter drum). The lines also indicate specific instruments on the drum set. This information is shown to you in Figure 2-2. Be certain to check back and review this legend when you begin playing drum set beats, fills, and solos. You will need to reference this information often, especially in the early stages.

Drummers must be experts with rhythm. After all, we *are* rhythmatists! In standard notation, a note is made up of a note head and a note stem. A note head is seen either as an empty circle (whole or half notes) or as a colored-in dot (all other notes). A note stem is a vertical line attached to the note head. Sometimes notes are connected or barred together by a single horizontal line—this is used to indicate eighth notes. Sometimes, you will see a double horizontal line—this is used to indicate sixteenth notes. Some single notes

FIGURE 2-2:
Drum set
legend

DRUM SET LEGEND

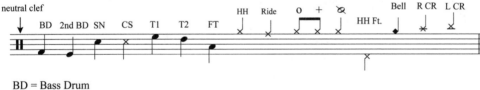

BD = Bass Drum
2nd BD= Second Bass Drum (double pedal or double kick)
SN= Snare Drum
CS = Cross Stick (on snare drum)
T1= High Tom-tom or Rack Tom 1
T2= Middle Tom-tom or Rack Tom 2
FT= Floor Tom-tom
HH=Hi-Hat (closed)
Ride= Ride Cymbal
o = Open Hi-Hat
+ = Closed Hi-Hat (used only when open HH patterns are present)
⋈= Half Open Hi-Hat (used for beats)
HH Ft.= Hi-hat Foot
Bell= Bell of the Ride Cymbal
R CR= Crash Cymbal Located on Your Right Side
L CR= Crash Cymbal Located on Your Left Side

have a wavy line that curves down the stem—this is called a flag. A single flag is used to signify single eighth notes. A double flag is used to signify single sixteenth notes. All of these note types are shown in Figure 2-3.

Notice that individual eighth notes look exactly the same as quarter notes, but with a flag attached to it. The individual sixteenth note also looks like the quarter note, but with two flags attached to it.

FIGURE 2-3:
Types of notes

Whole   Half   Quarter   Eighth   Two Eighths   Sixteenth   Two Sixteenths

Table of Notes

Standard notation is based on mathematics and follows the same rules as fractions. Figure 2-4 shows you the division of notes.

As you can see, notes divide into two equal parts. A whole note divides into two half notes; a half note divides into two quarter notes; a quarter note divides into two eighth notes; and an eighth note divides into two sixteenth notes. When making these divisions, a 1:2 ratio occurs between the whole and half note, the half and quarter note, the quarter and eighth note, and the eighth and sixteenth note.

FIGURE 2-4:
Divisional relationship of notes

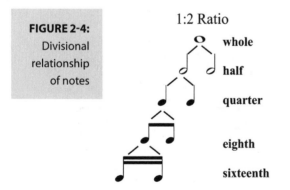

1:2 Ratio

whole

half

quarter

eighth

sixteenth

In the United Kingdom, notes have different names. A whole note is called a semibreve; a half note a minim; a quarter note a crochet; an eighth note a quaver; and a sixteenth note a semiquaver. Don't be confused by this and, unless you live in England, avoid these terms.

The pie charts in Figures 2-5 through 2-8 show you the divisional relationship of notes.

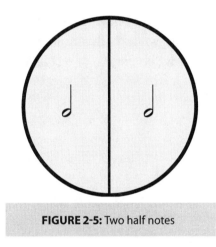

FIGURE 2-5: Two half notes

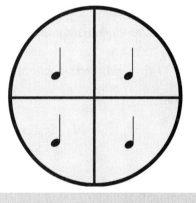

FIGURE 2-6: Four quarter notes

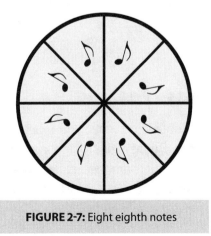

FIGURE 2-7: Eight eighth notes

FIGURE 2-8: Sixteen sixteenth notes

You can see that two half notes equals the whole pie; four quarter notes equals the whole pie; eight eighth notes equals the whole pie; and sixteen sixteenth notes equals the whole pie. This is the mathematical backbone of notation.

Reading Rests

Rests function exactly the same way as notes, but with one key difference: While a note signifies sound, a rest means silence. A rest does not mean to pause. The music continues whether you're resting or not (or whether there is sound or not). Think of a rest as a silent note.

When resting, always follow the music the same as if you were playing. Every note has a corresponding rest and rests have the same relationship to one another as notes do. Figure 2-9 shows each type of rest as it is divided from whole to sixteenth.

FIGURE 2-9:
Divisional relationship of rests

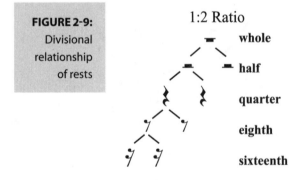

1:2 Ratio

whole

half

quarter

eighth

sixteenth

Time Signatures and Measures

Now that you have been exposed to notes and rests, you must piece them together to make rhythmical sentences. But in order to accomplish this, you must first learn about time signatures, which are also called meters. There are many time signatures used in music; however, most of this book will focus on 4/4, since rock is usually played in this meter.

FACT

Another name for 4/4 is common time. If you turn the radio on and flip through the stations, you will hear 4/4 used on most songs. No other time signature is so pervasive in music. Part of the reason for this is the symmetrical nature of 4/4: 2+2 is easy to dance or groove to.

All time signatures contain a top number and a bottom number. These numbers tell the musician two important things:

1. Number of beats in a measure
2. What note value equals one beat

You're probably asking yourself, "What's a beat, and what's a measure?" Most music is played in time; it has a pulse that, once started, continues until the composition or tune reaches its end. This pulse is the called the beat.

In written music, notes and rests are segmented into smaller compartments of time. These boxes of time are called measures or bars. In other words, notes and rests are contained within measures, and measure lines are used to mark each measure's borders. As you will see in Figure 2-10, measure lines—usually called bar lines—are simple vertical lines used to separate or partition music into "chunks" or "pieces" of time.

FIGURE 2-10:
Two measures
with bar line

Bar Line

You will notice in standard notation that there is no line dividing the two number fours of 4/4 time; the fours merely sit on top of one another. However, for educational purposes, temporarily accept 4/4 as a fraction.

All fractions have a top number, called a numerator, and a bottom number, called a denominator. The numerator tells you how many beats exist in a measure. Since there is a four in the numerator, you can say that there are four beats in each measure.

The denominator tells you what note value equals one beat. In order to find this, temporarily replace the numerator with a one. Now, you have 1/4, or a quarter. This tells you that the quarter note equals the beat. So what does 4/4 really mean? In this time signature, you have four beats in a measure and the quarter note represents (or equals) one beat.

Quarter and Eighth Notes

Quarter notes function as the pulse or beat in most of the music you will play in this book. In other words, the quarter note acts as the heartbeat of the music. When you place four quarter notes into a measure of 4/4, it is counted like Figure 2-11.

Each quarter note represents a downbeat. In 4/4, downbeats equal the numbers one, two, three, and four. If you divide quarter notes into eighth notes, you will have eight of them per measure. Figure 2-12 shows you one measure of eighth notes.

In Figure 2-12, the beat was divided into two parts. It should be counted "one-and, two-and, three-and, four-and." "Ands" are called upbeats. Upbeats represent the second half of a beat. Remember, for each note, there is a corresponding rest. In Figure 2-17, you'll get a chance to play eighth notes with eighth rests.

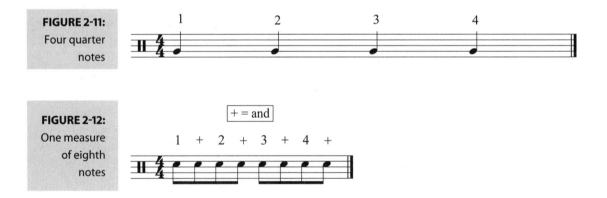

FIGURE 2-11:
Four quarter notes

FIGURE 2-12:
One measure of eighth notes

+ = and

Keeping Time and Counting Out Loud

One of the most important facets of music is timekeeping. Without a good internal clock, you will have limited ability to play with other musicians. Music exists in time and space. Time refers to the pulse of the music, while space refers to the rhythmical components (notes and rests) that exist within a time span.

All musicians should focus on timekeeping, but this is especially true of drummers, since you lay down the groove of the music. One of the best ways to improve your time is to count beats out loud. Professionals do not count out loud when they perform; however, counting is crucial in the practice room, especially for beginners. Counting will help you make sense of the rhythms you are reading.

As previously stated, when you see four quarter notes, you should count the downbeats 1, 2, 3, 4. Counting divisions and subdivisions is also helpful. For instance, you know that eighth notes are counted: one-and, two-and, three-and, four-and. Sixteenth notes are counted using the syllables: one-e-and-ah, two-e-and-ah, three-e-and-ah, four-e-and-ah. See Figure 2-13 for an illustration of this.

If you combine sixteenth notes and eighth notes, the rhythms become more elaborate. Moreover, if you use sixteenth rests, the rhythms really become knotty and difficult to play. When using these types of rests, you *must* be very diligent in your counting. Figure 2-14 shows you some common rhythmical patterns that use eighth note and sixteenth note combinations (examples A and B). This figure also shows you sixteenth note and sixteenth rest combinations (examples C, D, E, and F).

FIGURE 2-13:
Counting
sixteenth notes

FIGURE 2-14: Eighth notes, sixteenth notes, and sixteenth rests

Track 1

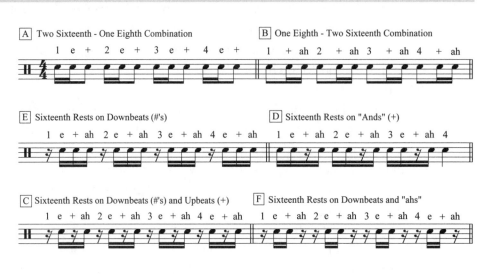

Playing Triplets

Triplets may seem complex at first, but soon they will become a natural extension of your musical vocabulary. There are four types of triplets. They are:

- Half-note triplets
- Quarter-note triplets
- Eighth-note triplets
- Sixteenth-note triplets (also called sextuplets)

Sometimes, three sixteenth-note triplets are joined together with an eighth note or two "regular" sixteenths, creating combination rhythms; variations on this are illustrated in Figure 2-16. Remember that *every* triplet has a corresponding rest, and in addition to the patterns detailed in Figure 2-16, triplets can be paired up with any duple pattern. (Duple patterns are rhythms that have two parts or rhythms that break down into groups of twos. For example, eighth notes have two parts—a downbeat and an upbeat—and sixteenth notes may be broken into two equal halves.) Many combinations of triple and duple rhythms can be made, and you are sure to come across them later in this book. For now though, you should concentrate on *how* triplets are played.

A half-note triplet divides a measure of 4/4 into three equal parts. Quarter-note triplets divide a measure of 4/4 into six equal parts. Eighth-note triplets divide a measure of 4/4 into twelve equal parts, and sixteenth-note triplets divide the beat into twenty-four equal parts.

Triplets are counted a number of ways. The best way to count them is: one-trip-let, two-trip-let, three-trip-let, four-trip-let. Sixteenth-note triplets are the only exception to this. At slower tempos, they are best counted: one-trip-let and-trip-let, two-trip-let and-trip-let, three-trip-let and trip-let, four-trip-let and-trip-let. At faster speeds, count sixteenth note triplets the same as you would count regular eighth notes (one-and, two-and, three-and, four-and).

Figure 2-15 shows you what each type of triplet looks like. Be sure to reference the audio CD if you're new to triplets. Listen to what these rhythms sound like when set against a metronome (see Chapter 19). On the CD, the metronome will play downbeats. In 4/4, downbeats are quarter notes and they are counted one, two, three, four. When you play half-note triplets with quarter notes, a polyrhythm is created called "three against four." (See Figure 2-15 A.)

FIGURE 2-15: Triplets

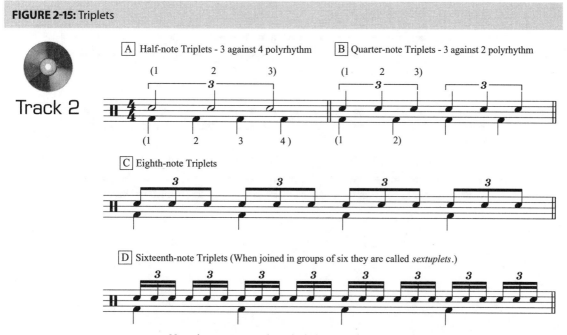

Track 2

Note: the quarter notes shown in the bottom space of the staff represent downbeats (#'s)!

Polyrhythms are two or more equally spaced, independent, rhythmical patterns superimposed over each other. This layering creates a complex rhythmical cycle. The patterns usually begin together on the first downbeat. However, they quickly move apart until they reach the end of the cycle.

When quarter-note triplets are played with regular quarter notes, another polyrhythm, called "three against two," is formed. In this case, three triplets layer over two quarter notes on beats 1 and 2. The polyrhythm cycles around again for beats 3 and 4. (See Figure 2-15 B.) Eighth-note and sixteenth-note triplets *do not* create polyrhythms when played with a quarter-note pulse in 4/4. Therefore, they are the easiest to conceptualize. (See Figure 2-15 C and D.)

FIGURE 2-16: Combination rhythms using triplets, eighth notes, and sixteenths notes

Track 3

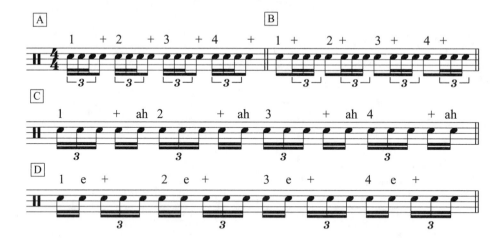

Reading Exercises #1 and #2

Reading Exercise #1 (Figure 2-17) is geared toward advanced-beginners and Reading Exercise #2 (Figure 2-18) is geared toward intermediate-level drummers. As stated earlier, if you've never read music before, you will need to start with simpler notational exercises. Reading Exercise #1 uses whole notes, half notes, half rests, quarter notes, quarter rests, eighth notes; and eighth rests. Reading Exercise #2 focuses on eighth notes; eighth rests; sixteenth notes; sixteenth rests; half-, quarter-, eighth-, and sixteenth-note triplets; and triple-duple combinations. On measure fifteen, you will see half-note triplets. Quarter-note triplets have been written in parenthesis above the staff to help you conceptualize the half-note triplets. In order to play half-note triplets in time, you should count quarter-note triplets. Half-note triplets line up with their quarter note brethren *every other note*.

Reading Exercises #1 and #2 are designed for the snare drum or drum pad. Since they're rather lengthy, you should learn them in segments or phrases. The first exercise is formatted into four measure lines for a reason. When practicing this piece, tackle only four measures at a time. (If this is too much, try two measures!) Once you feel comfortable playing four-bar phrases, try playing eight-bar phrases. Continue this approach until you've glued the entire piece together. This same methodology should also be applied to Reading Exercise #2. For this piece, however, you may want to focus on only three measures at a time (line by line). Once you're comfortable with this, add bars (or lines) until you've pieced the entire exercise together. This gradual, little-by-little method works every time.

ESSENTIAL

Whole and half notes are not used very often in drum music. This is because drums do not have sustaining options. In other words, drummers cannot hold a note out like a trumpeter, violinist, or singer. Despite this, you still need to be familiar with whole and half notes, since they are used in conjunction with rolls.

When practicing these etudes, remember the following rules of thumb:

- **Count off before playing.** This means choosing an appropriate tempo (probably moderately slow). The tempo markings on both pieces are fairly slow. Nonetheless, choose a speed that best suits *your* needs. Be sure you count off and play at the same tempo. Playing and counting off at unrelated tempos is common with novices, so use a metronome to ensure congruity and exactness.

- **Count out loud while you play.** It's time to overcome your shyness! Unless you're adept at reading music, counting aloud is a must. Why? It will help you improve your rhythmical accuracy. Counting is the key to rendering rhythms correctly. If you don't count aloud, you might skip over rests, drop beats, or lose the pulse of the music.

- **Use the correct posture and grasp(s) when playing and reading music.** This will be detailed in Chapter 3.

- **Take a moment to reflect on the pros and cons of each run-through.** Ask yourself: Did I count off? Was the time steady? Did I play the correct rhythms? Did I observe each rest? Did I play the indicated stickings? If you answered "No" to any of the above, go back and try again. Practice, as they say, makes perfect...or at least close to perfect.

FIGURE 2-17: Reading Exercise #1

Track 4

This etude uses whole notes, half notes, half rests, quarter notes, quarter rests, eighth notes, and eighth rests.

FIGURE 2-18: Reading Exercise #2

Track 5

Be sure to alternate sticking (R, L, R, L, etc.) throughout!

Chapter 3
Snare Drum Technique

This chapter is dedicated to snare drum technique. You cannot be a good drum set player if you are a poor snare drummer. Therefore, the following pages detail stick grasps, how to get a good sound, rudiments, and other technical exercises. This chapter will show you how to develop speed, control, and articulation, all of which you will apply to the drum set in later chapters.

Stick Control

If you're an excellent snare drummer, you will automatically play drum sets with more precision, dexterity, endurance, efficiency, and rhythmical accuracy.

Too often, rock drummers avoid stick-control studies. However, by circumventing snare drum or "pad" work, you only take the easy way out and you will limit your ability to accurately play intermediate-to-advanced beats, fills, and solos.

No truly great drum set player has poor stick control. But how do you get it? In order to play the drum set well, you must spend time with your snare drum (or a practice pad) and train your hands to play a variety of stickings and rhythmical patterns. You must also focus on creating a good sound; this is a subtle art form all by itself.

The fundamental goal with stick control is to build and hone your gross- and fine-motor skills. This can be broken down into three categories:

1. Wrist development
2. Finger development
3. Arm development

Your wrists are quite versatile; they can be used to play slow, fast, loud, and soft. In order to use them, you must turn your hand in a "palm-flat" position, which is described later in this chapter. Once in a palm-flat position, you will move your hands up and down—using the small bones of the wrist—as if mimicking a doggie paddle.

Your fingers and arms are less multipurposed. However, they still play a vital role in any playing context. The fingers, for example, are best employed with playing extremely fast rhythms. On the downside, they cannot be used to play loud accents or thunderous patterns.

For most drum students, finger development is quite difficult and requires a lot of focused practice. In order to use the fingers properly, you will want to place your hand in a "thumbs-up" position, use Fulcrum #1, and twitch your fingers as if cupping your palm. (In case you were wondering, the terms *Fulcrum #1* and *thumbs up* are described later in this chapter!)

The arms play a pivotal role in navigating around the drum set. In terms of stick control, the forearms are used for extremely loud accents or other forceful playing. On the downside, the arms are too cumbersome to play soft, intricate rhythmical patterns. They're best used to add explosiveness to your playing.

There are two basic arm techniques. One is called the straight-forearm throw. This is used for multiple accents or a series of very loud notes. When using this technique, you will play from the elbow and lock your wrists. This is a very rigid technique and should be used sparingly. (Most musical situations do not require constant use of straight-forearm throws.)

The second technique is an arm-whipping motion. This is used for single strong accents. In order to play this, you point your elbow away from your body. Then, using a sudden whipping motion, you snap the stick down onto the head. As you do this, your wrist must be flexible and loose until it locks into place at the end of the stroke.

Ultimately, it is the integration of the wrists, fingers, and arms that allow the drummer to play an assortment of complex rhythms and patterns. As you develop wrist, finger, and arm techniques, you will naturally learn when and how to employ each skill. When you practice, you must always keep your muscles relaxed. Tension in your hands, wrists, arms, and shoulders will interfere with your ability to play "phat" grooves as well as intricate rhythms.

Holding the Sticks

The first step in developing stick control is learning how to properly hold a pair of sticks. In this book, you will learn how to play matched grip. Many students and teachers think that your match-grip grasp should be fixed or unmovable. This is incorrect, at least from the perspective of a drum set player. Your grasp should indeed change based on what you're playing. As you will learn, there are two Fulcrums, and the skillful drummer knows how to toggle back and forth between these two grasps with ease.

Figures 3-1 and 3-2 show you what matched and traditional grips look like, respectively. You can see that traditional grip is very different in the left hand.

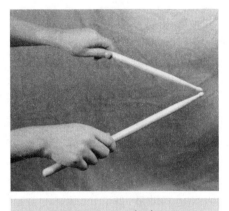

FIGURE 3-1: Matched grip

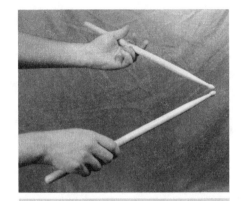

FIGURE 3-2: Traditional grip

This book will not concentrate on traditional grip since it's harder to learn and less popular among contemporary drummers and percussionists. However, drummers such as Stewart Copeland, Vinnie Colaiuta, and newcomer Keith Carlock continue to keep this grip alive. Also, many jazz drummers play "trad," since it's very nuance oriented.

Below are the steps you need to take to learn how to play matched grip:

1. Stand with your arms at your side in a natural, comfortable position. Notice how your fingers curl slightly upward.
2. Lift your arms at the elbows (not the shoulders) until your arms each form a right angle.
3. Turn your wrists so that you can see the four knuckles of your index, middle, ring, and pinky fingers. In other words, your palm should face the floor. This hand position is known as palm flat, and it is similar to the German timpani grip.

   You will use this position to play on the snare drum and the rack tom positioned just above the snare. When riding on your cymbal and hi-hat, playing your floor tom-tom, or when playing very fast single-stroke rolls, it's common to turn your thumb upward. This hand position is known as thumbs up, and it is similar to French timpani grip.

4. Once your hand is positioned, pick up the drumsticks and hold them between the pad of your thumb and the first joint nearer your fingertip. This book will refer to this grasp as Fulcrum #1. When in this position, the middle, ring, and pinky fingers should rest gently on the sticks. Additionally, the middle finger is used to subtly balance each stick. Also, when holding the sticks, never let your pinky finger point outward. This afternoon teatime pose is a common error.

Fulcrums are simply pressure points. Pressure refers to the amount of weight you pinch between the thumb and index fingers. Like a door hinge, Fulcrums keep the sticks in a stationary playing position. An alternate Fulcrum—used primarily for slower and less complex rhythms—is created between the second joint (moving away from your fingertip) and the pad of the thumb. In this book, this grasp will be called Fulcrum #2. In a drum set context, you will need to switch often between Fulcrums #1 and #2 depending on what you're playing.

E ALERT!

You must always use a proper Fulcrum when you play. Never let the sticks fall back into the third joint of the fingers or the web of the hand. When this occurs, the sticks sit in your hand like a club and stick control is impossible. Likewise, if your index finger and thumb touch, your Fulcrum has come undone.

If you're having a hard time determining when to use Fulcrum #1 versus Fulcrum #2, remember that Fulcrum #1 is used for sharp, articulated rhythms; Fulcrum #2 is used for less intricate, slow rhythms. Also, Fulcrum #1 is always used to play a buzz roll (see Figure 3-7).

Figure 3-3 shows you what Fulcrum #1 looks like. For now, this is

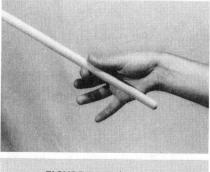

FIGURE 3-3: Fulcrum #1

the only Fulcrum you should use. Later on, you will learn where to apply Fulcrum #2.

Getting a Good Sound

Whether you're playing on a snare drum, pad, tom-toms, cymbals, or any other instrument, the first rule of thumb for getting a good sound is to stay relaxed. If your body is tense or you are holding the stick tightly, you will not make a good sound. Take a drumstick and strike it on any hard surface (like a chair or floor). As you do it, clamp the stick as tightly as possible. Then hold the stick as loosely as you can and strike the same surface. You will hear a big difference.

When you hold the stick loosely, you will hear the pitch of the stick itself and you will hear the wood of the stick vibrating. When you hold the stick tightly, you will only hear a dead thud. In a real context, you will want to hold the sticks as loosely as possible.

Always let the sticks rebound, or bounce, after you strike a drum. Bounce allows you to play smoothly and effortlessly at all speeds, but especially fast tempos. When you snap a stick down with a relaxed grip, the stick should bounce back on its own. Harness this energy with every stroke. In other words, let the natural law of action and reaction work for you.

Beware of the signs that you're playing too stiffly. For instance, if you never, ever drop a stick when you're playing, you're probably grasping too tightly. Obviously, you don't want to be fumbling your sticks, but an occasional drop is actually a good sign that you're playing in a relaxed manner.

Accuracy is another key factor in getting a good sound. If your snare drum head looks like someone was pelting it with a BB gun, you're probably not playing very accurately. A professional drummer's snare head will wear only in a small cylindrical area about the size of a bull's eye. This is a sign of good aim. The better your aim, the more consistent your sound will be.

Additionally, if you're playing in the "sweet" spot on the head, your sound will also contain the perfect balance of overtones, resonance, and fundamental pitch. The sweet spot on a snare drum is slightly off center; the exact center is dead sounding. The best policy is to aim slightly above the center of the drum. For very soft playing, you should move toward the rim itself in varying degrees. Figure 3-4 shows you the sweet spot on the snare head. Notice that the sticks create an upside-down "V" shape.

FIGURE 3-4:
Proper striking area on the snare drum

Tuning and equipment also play a significant role in getting a good sound. See Chapters 4 and 19 respectively for information on these very important topics.

Developing Technique

Rudiments are the backbone of drumming and they should be integrated into your daily practice routine. The history of rudiments is detailed in *The Everything® Drums Book,* so this publication will focus more on rudimental applications. The most exhaustive list of rudiments comes from the Percussion Arts Society (PAS). You can go to their website, *www.pas.org,* and download their rudiment list for free. PAS lists forty internationally recognized rudiments. The original list, created in the United States by the National Association of Rudimental Drummers (NARD), contained only twenty-six.

Charley Wilcoxon's legendary book, *Modern Rudimental Swing Solos for the Advanced Drummer,* is a must have for anyone interested in developing great rudimental "chops." Not only does this book list rudiments and variations, each snare drum solo provides an unbeatable technical workout. Standout pieces include, "Rolling in Rhythm," "Heating the Rudiments," and "Three Camps."

The most important rudiments are:

- Single-stroke roll
- Double-stroke roll (also called a long roll)
- Single paradiddle
- Flam
- Three-stroke ruff (also called a drag)
- Buzz roll (also called a multiple-bounce roll or orchestral roll)

If you know these rudiments, you will be ready to learn all of the others. This is because all rudiments fall into the following categories: single-stroke roll rudiments, multiple-bounce roll rudiments, double-stroke rudiments, diddle rudiments, flam rudiments, and drag rudiments.

The Six Basic Rudiments

In Figure 3-7, you will see the six essential rudiments. The single-stroke roll uses an alternating sticking of right, left, right, left. This rudiment, like all of the rolls, must be played slowly at first. Eventually, you should speed up the roll until it actually sounds like a drum roll. In order to do this, you must play steady and consistent strokes. Be patient along the way. Steadiness and consistency are much more important than speed. Proper form, rhythmical accuracy, and correct sticking always come first. If you're a conscientious student, speed will develop naturally over time.

The double-stroke roll is the granddaddy of them all. This ubiquitous rudiment sounds similar to the single-stroke roll; however, the sticking is right, right, left, left. Sometimes teachers call this the "mama, dada" rudiment, which is onomatopoeia for the way the rudiment sounds when played. The first note is called the primary stroke and the second note is called the secondary stroke. In other words, the roll cycle breaks down to: R (primary), R (secondary), L (primary), L (secondary). The primary stroke should be a snap of the wrist; the secondary stroke uses a controlled bounce.

The single paradiddle is nothing more than a combination of the single-stroke roll and the double-stroke roll. In this case, you will play: right, left, right, right, left, right, left, left. This is a confusing sticking to beginners. However, with a little practice, it will feel quite natural. Don't forget to play the accent (>) found at the beginning of each paradiddle. An accent is a dynamic emphasis.

The flam employs control strokes (see below) and very definite stick heights. This rudiment contains two types of notes: a grace note and a main note. The grace note is never counted, and it is written in small print. The main note is the counted rhythm. Grace notes may be paired up with any type of main note, including quarter notes, eighth notes, sixteenth notes, triplets, and others.

The Flam and Three-Stroke Ruff

Alternating flams are best played using the wrists. The hand that plays the grace note must be in a down position. This means that the wrist is straight and the stick hovers about 1" above the drumhead. The hand that plays the main note must be in an up position. This means that the wrist is bent and the thumb points upward.

Do not attempt a flam until your hands are in the proper positions. When you strike the drum, the hand assigned to the main note plays a down stroke. A down stroke simply means that you snap the stick downward then stop it from bouncing back up. By playing a down stroke, your hand falls into position to play the next flam. In other words, the hand that played the main note is now in position to play a grace note. The hand assigned to the grace note does the exact opposite. This hand plays a tap, followed by an up stroke. After you tap the drum, the wrist is used to gently raise the stick into an up position. Down strokes and up strokes are collectively called control strokes. See Figures 3-5 and 3-6 to better understand the stick heights you need to use when playing flams.

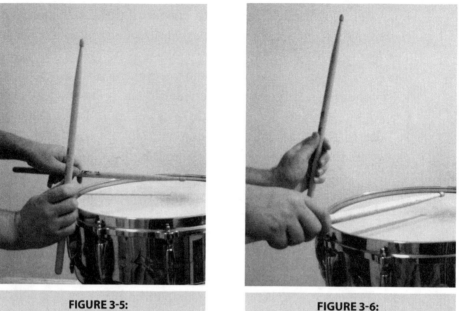

| **FIGURE 3-5:** | **FIGURE 3-6:** |
| Stick position for a right flam | Stick position for a left flam |

If you start in an up position, snap a stick down, and allow it to return to its original position, you're playing a full stroke. Similarly, if you place the stick approximately 6" above the head, snap it down, and allow it to return to its original position, you're playing a half stroke. While very useful, these strokes are not used when playing alternating flams or ruffs.

The three-stroke ruff uses the exact same principle as flams. Again, proper stick heights are essential here and you must use down strokes, taps, and up strokes. The only difference is that now you will play two grace notes. When you play the grace notes or taps, you should use a delicate bounce followed by an upward motion in the wrist. Play the two grace notes using the same kind of wrist snap and bounce you used for the double-stroke roll.

FIGURE 3-7: The big six rudiments

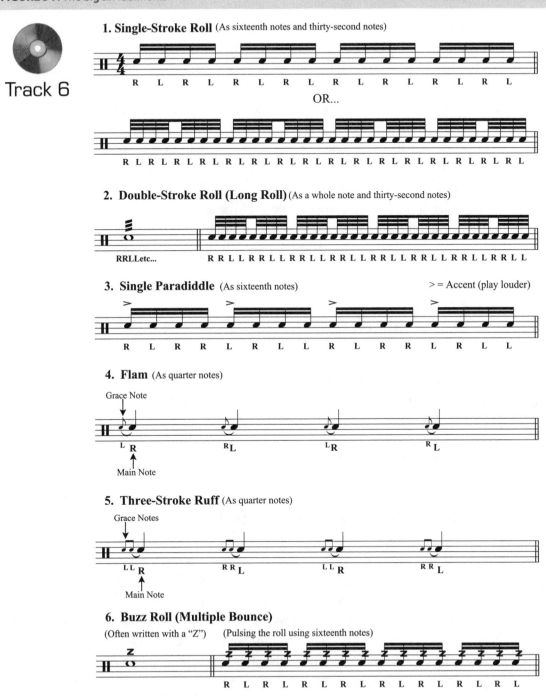

Track 6

1. Single-Stroke Roll (As sixteenth notes and thirty-second notes)

R L R L R L R L R L R L R L R L

OR...

R L R L R L R L R L R L R L R L R L R L R L R L R L R L R L R L

2. Double-Stroke Roll (Long Roll) (As a whole note and thirty-second notes)

RRLLetc...

R R L L R R L L R R L L R R L L R R L L R R L L R R L L R R L L

3. Single Paradiddle (As sixteenth notes)

> = Accent (play louder)

R L R R L R L L R L R R L R L L

4. Flam (As quarter notes)

Grace Note

L R R L L R R L

Main Note

5. Three-Stroke Ruff (As quarter notes)

Grace Notes

L L R R R L L L R R R L

Main Note

6. Buzz Roll (Multiple Bounce)

(Often written with a "Z") (Pulsing the roll using sixteenth notes)

R L R L R L R L R L R L R L R L

Note: With any of these rudiments, you may also lead off with the left hand!

The Buzz Roll

The goal with the buzz roll or multiple-stroke roll is to create a seamless "shhhhhhhh" sound on the drumhead. In order to do this, you need to pinch the sticks a little tighter using Fulcrum #1. You then press the sticks into the head and use your middle (and sometimes ring) fingers to initiate and control a series of short, tight buzzes. The key to creating a smooth roll lies in the underlying rhythm. To get an even, unbroken sound, move your wrists using fast sixteenth notes or triplets rhythms. Concentrate on creating uniform buzzes. While it's impossible to count the number of bounces you will create, listen for consistency and homogeneity. In Figure 3-7 you will see the buzz written both as a whole-note roll (the way you will see it notated in real music) and with underlying sixteenth notes. Be sure to listen to all of the above-mentioned rudiments on the accompanying CD to hear how they should sound.

Other Technical Studies

In addition to rudiments, there are other technical exercises you should practice. George Lawrence Stone, his student Joe Morello, and others have written books that focus on stick control and hand technique (see Appendix A). When used creatively, the exercises in these books can also be applied to the drum set.

As a beginner or intermediate drummer, it's highly recommended that you spend a large portion of each practice session focusing on stick control. Stick control separates the real drummers from the guys who just bang around. It's very tempting to spend most of your time learning how to play songs by your favorite bands. It's also tempting to simply "jam" for an hour and call that practicing. However, if you circumvent technical exercises in your daily routine, you will never play at your full potential. It's really that simple. See Figure 3-8 for an introduction to stick control from a nonrudimental perspective. Stick-control exercises are all about combinations, permutations, and variations, so you will also want to become familiar with all of the stick-control books recommended in Appendix A. When playing Figure 3-8, heed the advice on page 42.

FIGURE 3-8: Stick control exercises

1. Velocity Exercise - This exercise will help you develop speed and finger control!

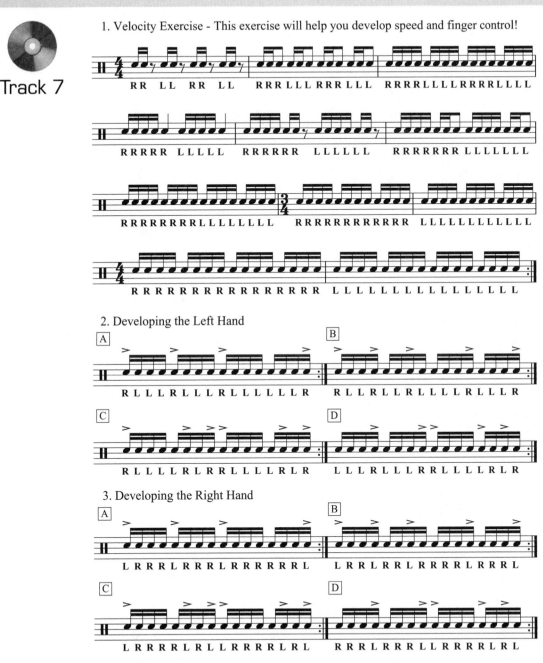

Track 7

RR LL RR LL   RRRLLLRRRLLL   RRRRLLLLRRRRLLLL

RRRRR LLLLL   RRRRRR   LLLLLL   RRRRRRR LLLLLLL

RRRRRRRLLLLLLLL   RRRRRRRRRRRR   LLLLLLLLLLLL

RRRRRRRRRRRRRRRR   LLLLLLLLLLLLLLLL

2. Developing the Left Hand

A
RLLLRLLLRLLLLLR

B
RLLRLLRLLLLRLLLR

C
RLLLLRLRRLLLLRLR

D
LLLRLLLRRLLLLRLR

3. Developing the Right Hand

A
LRRRLRRRLRRRRRL

B
LRRLRRLRRRRLRRRL

C
LRRRRLRLLRRRRLRL

D
RRRLRRRLLRRRRLRL

Note: These are samples of the kinds of exercises you can practice. Many more permutations can be created!

Instructions for playing Figure 3-8:

- Loop each pattern many times. (Play each exercise for at least a couple of minutes.)
- Follow stickings very closely.
- Play strong accents (where applicable).
- Play slowly at first, then gradually increase the tempo.
- Use a metronome to ensure steadiness.
- At fast speeds, incorporate your fingers.

Chapter 4
The Drum Set

This chapter describes the drum set, including its parts, how to set it up, how to tune it, and how to maintain it. You will also learn about bass-drum techniques and begin playing the kit. Most of all, you will have a chance to play exercises designed to jump-start limb integration and limb independence. Four-way coordination is a critical skill in drumming. To play beats, fills, and solos, you will need to train your hands and feet to play complex layers of rhythms. This chapter shows you how to begin this very detailed process.

The Drum Set

The drum set is a collection of many instruments and apparatuses. Before you play your drums, you should become familiar with each component. It's also important for you to know how each component is pieced together. The major parts of the drum set are:

- Drums
- Cymbals
- Hardware
- Pedals
- Other accessories

Each of these items contains parts of their own. For example, drums are comprised of a shell (wooden or metal), hoops (sometimes called rims), drumheads (also called skins), key rods (used to tension the heads), and lugs (threaded casings that hold the key rods in place). On a snare drum, you will also see snare wires on the bottom head and a "throw-off" lever. This is used to pull the snare wires taut against the head, or alternately, release them, creating a "snare's off" timbale sound.

Cymbals are round metallic plates that contain a bell and a bowed edge. They are made out of copper and tin-based alloys, and production techniques can vary greatly. In fact, the process of cymbal making is a delicate art form, not unlike sword making or other metallurgical sciences. Cymbal making includes smelting, forging, hammering, lathing, and polishing. There is a growing interest in hand-made cymbals. Arguably, the finest traditional cymbal manufacturer is Bosphorus, a small Turkish company that specializes in centuries-old hand-hammered techniques.

Hardware refers to the chrome stands that suspend the cymbals and drums. Stands can vary greatly. For instance, cymbals stands come in an assortment of styles and design. Some contain single-braced legs; others are double braced. Some are boom stands; others are straight stands. Similarly, snare drum stands and tom-tom mounts come in all shapes and sizes. Some tom mounts, for example, clip onto the drums; others attach through a hole in the shell.

There are two types of pedals on a standard drum set: the hi-hat pedal and the bass-drum pedal. Both are spring-loaded apparatuses, which usually include a chain-pull mechanism. Sometimes a second bass-drum pedal is added to the kit, as you will learn in Chapter 13. Also, Latin drum set players sometimes use pedals hooked up to cow bells. A bass-drum pedal(s) clamps onto the bass-drum hoop(s); the hi-hat pedal is a freestanding apparatus. When you push down on the hi-hat pedal, the hi-hat cymbals create either a "splash" sound or a "chick" sound. The latter is more common and you will often hear drummers referring to hi-hat foot patterns as hi-hat "chicks."

Other accessories on the drum set might include Latin percussion instruments such as cowbells, wood blocks, and hand drums. You might also see drummers using an auxiliary hi-hat and or snare (often a piccolo model drum). Also, gongs, electronics pads, and even timpani may be used to augment traditional setups.

Setting Up Your Drums

Setup affects your playing in ways you may not even be aware of. Moreover, you can usually tell if a drummer is good or not simply based on setup. If you see a neat, orderly, and ergonomic drum kit, it's probably safe to assume that the drummer is at least a thoughtful musician. On the other hand, beginners usually have no idea how to position their drums and cymbals. Consequently, their understandably questionable playing is compromised even further.

The first, and most important, aspect of your setup is the position of the drum throne in reference to the bass-drum pedal, the hi-hat pedal, and the snare drum. When you sit at the kit, the throne height should be such that your legs bend at right angles; slightly obtuse is also okay. The snare drum should be positioned between your legs two to three inches below the belly button. If the drum height is too low, your hands will brush up against your thighs while playing. If it's set too high, you will find that you're mistakenly hitting the rim or elevating your shoulders unnaturally. The snare should also be flat. If you angle your snare too much, you will end up swiping at the drum. You will also not be able to play rim shots.

Setting up your tom-toms correctly is also paramount. The high-rack tom (T1) should be placed approximately 1" above your snare drum at a slight angle. If you use a second-rack tom (T2), you should place it flush with your high tom, about 1" apart.

The floor tom should be positioned a few inches below your snare drum, at a slight angle toward you.

The height of the hi-hat may change depending on what you're playing. If you're playing loud, heavy rock, you will want to raise the hi-hat so you can "get under it," as it were, and dig into the edge of the cymbals. With a higher hi-hat, you can also create a larger spread between your hands, allowing you to strike the snare drum with greater force. On the other hand, if you're playing softer music, you may wish to ride on top of the hi-hat cymbals. In this case, you should position the hi-hat lower to the snare drum.

On a five-piece kit, the ride cymbal(s) should be positioned above the floor tom. Place it on an angle, in a comfortable position, so that your arm is extended about three-quarters its total length. Basically, you want to be able to strike the edge, the bell, and the bow of the cymbal with ease. Like the hi-hat, crash cymbals can be positioned differently depending on the style of music you are playing. The same principles described for the hi-hat also apply to crash cymbals. The louder you play, the higher you should position the cymbals. However, be careful not to place them too high and out of reach. If you're literally jumping up out of your drum throne to crash, you need to lower your cymbals.

FIGURE 4-1: Five-piece drum set

Figure 4-1 shows you a typical five-piece drum kit setup.

Tuning the Drums

Tuning your drums is a critical part of being a drummer. If your drums are out of tune, you will not be able to play your best. Moreover, if you're performing, the audience will not get a clear picture of what it is you're playing if your drums are tensioned poorly. However, with a little know-how, you can make even a cheaply made drum kit sound passable.

There are some basic rules to tuning that apply to all drums. If you're putting a new head on a drum, you need to first remove the drum from the kit so that you can work more efficiently and don't get a sympathetic ring from the other drums as you tune. Using a drum key, remove the old head. Then use a dry rag to remove any debris or dust that has accumulated around the inside of the shell and along the drum's bearing edge. Next, place the drumhead on the shell and spin it to make sure the lip of the head hangs evenly over the drum. After this, place the hoop or rim over the drumhead and make sure it sits evenly on top of the drum. If you find that the hoop is warped or bent, you'll need to buy a new one. Bent hoops cannot fasten a head to a drum very well. The result is a terrible sound, and you will become very frustrated when tuning.

ALERT!

When you begin tuning, you may hear a crackle noise. Don't worry! The head is not ripping or tearing; this is just the sound of the Mylar film being stretched. After a few turns, the head will begin to tension and conform to the shell and the crackling will cease.

After you've placed the hoop on top of the head, screw in the tension rods (also known as key rods) using your fingers. At this point, the head has been seated properly and you are ready to actually begin tuning. Pick any tension rod, and using a drum key, turn the rod clockwise two 360° rotations. Now move to the rod directly opposite and do the same thing. Next, go to the tension rod either to the right or left of the original rod and turn it two full revolutions; then move the rod on its opposite side and twist it two full rotations. Continue this process until each tension rod has been

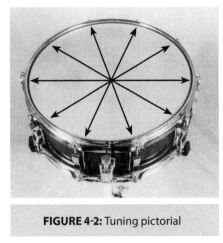

FIGURE 4-2: Tuning pictorial

turned two clockwise 360° revolutions. Make sure you always tune using opposites, and make sure you rotate each rod equally. This is the secret to success. Figure 4-2 illustrates how to properly compass up a drum.

Once the drum begins to resemble a pitch, tuning becomes more subjective. Before you start thinking about pitch though, you should check your tuning accuracy. To do this, softly tap around the edges of the drum and listen to each pitch. Sometimes the drum's overtones are distracting when doing this. If this occurs, press down slightly in the middle of the head so you can hear the fundamental pitch more clearly.

Use this general approach for tuning all of your drums. When working with double-headed drums, as a rule, you should keep the bottom head tighter than the top head. The bottom head plays a greater role in determining pitch than you might think. This is especially true of the nonbeater head on a bass drum.

All drums are different and every drum seems to have a distinct personality. Because of this, you will need to experiment with the pitch relationship between the top and bottom heads in order to reduce unwanted overtones, ring, and warble. Remember, the better your drums sound, the better you will sound.

Caring for Your Drums

Like any instrument, proper care and maintenance is crucial to your drum and cymbal longevity. If you're lax about taking care of your gear, you will not get the most out of it. In fact, likely, it will break down, fall apart, strip, or malfunction in unforeseen ways.

The first step in taking care of your equipment is to be mindful of storage. Water is the enemy to any instrument. Often, drummers keep their kits in basements or damp cellars. Needless to say, these rooms are not conducive to the health of instruments. Therefore, be sure to choose a dry area to store your gear. Also, always avoid very hot zones in your home, like in front of a radiator, or extreme cold areas, like an unheated garage in the wintertime.

FACT

In order to protect your hardware from stripping, don't overtighten your stands. You also should not overtighten the wing nuts on top of your cymbal stands. If you do, you will not only choke your cymbals, you will also run the risk of cracking them. After you crash a cymbal, it must have room to vibrate, rise, and fall.

Second, always carry your gear (particularly drums) in cases when traveling. The myth persists that since you hit drums they are somehow impervious. However, it's easy to nick or ding up drum shells when carrying them without some sort of protective covering. Hard shell cases are the best, and they should be used if you're doing extensive travel, especially on airplanes. If you are flying and are checking your drums, you should consider Anvil Cases. These are the sturdiest cases on the market. On the downside, all hard shell cases add bulk and extra weight. For this reason, soft "gig bags" are okay for local travel as long as you're still careful transferring them from one location to the next.

Bass Drum Techniques

The drum set player has two pedals to contend with. They are the bass-drum and hi-hat pedals. In Chapter 13, you will learn how to play double kick, but for now, you need to focus on a single bass-drum pedal.

There are four bass drum techniques you should know. The first uses the ankle to manipulate the beater while the heel is firmly planted on the footboard of the pedal. The second uses the ball of the foot and toes in a fixed position. The third uses the ball of your foot and toes in a sliding position, and the fourth uses the whole foot and the leg in a kind of leg drop.

To play the ankle-heel technique, or heel's-down technique, rest your heel on the footboard of the pedal and tap the ball of your foot. This will move the beater to strike the head of the bass drum. After each tap, let the beater retract; do not bury the beater into the drumhead. For all of the bass drum techniques described here, keep your foot in constant contact with the footboard. For this specific technique, you must also keep your heel in a fixed position. The ankle-heel, or heel's-down, technique can be used for very soft to medium-loud playing and for slow to fast playing. Furthermore, you can apply this technique to the hi-hat foot.

The next position is often called a heel's-up technique. This requires you to lift your leg and play with the ball of your foot together with your toes. This technique can be used for groove playing. In other words, it can be used to play most rock beats. However, the tendency is to plant the bass drum beater into the drumhead when using this technique, and these types of "dead strokes" should generally be avoided. The heel's-up technique is best used for loud single notes, usually when combined with the hands. For example, you might play sixteenth or thirty-second notes in the hands. As you do this, you might place select subdivisions in the kick drum. (Subdivision refers to the notational breakdown of rhythms from quarter to eighths to sixteenths, etc.)

ESSENTIAL

Another common rhythm uses fast triplets broken up between the hands and the bass drum. In this context, the heel's-up position is great to use when playing two triplets in the hands and one triplet in the bass drum. You may also apply this technique to the hi-hat foot for similar rhythmical applications.

The third technique uses the heel's-up technique together with a foot slide. This could be called a heel's up-foot slide. This technique is used for two consecutive notes in the kick drum (usually played very fast and very loud). To play the foot slide, place the ball of your foot about half way up the footboard. This is the position for the first note. For the second note, you will slide up the footboard, causing the beater to strike the head. After you strike the second note, the foot must return to its original position (half way up the footboard). Sliding from note to note allows you to play very fast, successive notes in a relaxed, flowing manner.

The last technique uses a full leg drop. This requires you to actually lift your leg from your hip then drop it down, creating a loud tone on the bass drum. This technique is similar to the heel's-up method, except that you play with much greater force. When you play the leg drop, do not take your foot off of the footboard. Instead, allow it to hover above it with the sole of your foot touching the pedal. After you strike the drum, let the beater retract. Then, raise your leg in preparation for another drop. Use this technique for less complex rhythms (like eighth notes) in a loud context.

It's best to learn all of these techniques gradually. For now, practice Figure 4-3 using the ankle-heel (also called heel's down) technique only. As you move through this book, you will learn when to apply the other bass drum techniques detailed here.

FIGURE 4-3:
Bass drum
exercises

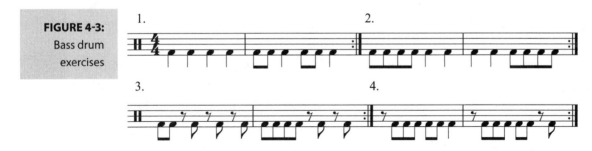

Repeat each exercise on loop at various tempos. Try adding the hi-hat foot on beats 2 and 4!

Basic Patterns to Get You Started

The exercises shown in Figure 4-4 are easy patterns designed to get you started on the drum set. These are not "rock" beats per se. Rather, they are four-way coordination patterns designed to get you exploring both limb integration and limb independence. Exercise #1 uses only the feet. Here, you will move back and forth (using quarter notes) between the bass drum and the hi-hat foot. Exercise #2 uses the bass drum on all four downbeats and the hi-hat foot on beats two and four. Exercise #3 shifts back and forth between the bass drum and the snare. Exercise #4 keeps the snare drum on beats two and four, but the bass drum now plays all four downbeats. Exercise #5 is mostly the same as Exercise #4; the only difference is that the hi-hat foot now plays on beats two and four. In Exercise #6, the bass drum, snare, hi-hat foot, and ride cymbal all become active. Here, you move in a right, left, right, left manner. This means that on beats one and three, you will play the ride cymbal with the right hand and the bass drum with the right foot. On beats two and four, you will play the snare drum with the left hand and the hi-hat with the left foot. When you do this, you're moving back and forth from the right side of your body to the left side of your body. (This assumes your drums are set up in a right-handed position. If you are a lefty, the pattern will simply reverse so that you are playing in a left, right, left, right manner.)

The last pattern, Exercise #7, combines the snare drum (left hand) and the bass drum (right foot) on beats one and three. On beats two and four, you will play the ride cymbal (right hand) with the hi-hat foot (left foot). In drumming, the tendency is to think and feel drum parts like exercise #6; your inclination will be to play in a symmetrical right-to-left or left-to-right fashion. However, mixing your limbs so the left hand plays with the right foot and the right hand plays with the left foot is a little trickier. This requires coordination and is the beginning of limb independence, the hallmark of pro-level drum set playing.

As you play these patterns, and most of the rock beats featured in this book, you may employ a looser grip that this publication calls Fulcrum #2. This grip may be used for any beat as long as it does not contain buzzes, sixteenth notes, thirty-second notes, or sextuplets at *fast* speeds. For highly technical patterns, like fast single or double stroke rolls, Fulcrum #1 is often desired; see Chapter 3. Only you can determine when you've crossed the tempo threshold where Fulcrum #2 feels "sloppy" and Fulcrum #1 must be implemented. As is usually the case, musical context will determine your choice of Fulcrum.

To use Fulcrum #2, you will hold the stick in between the pad of your thumb and the second knuckle (or notch) in your forefinger (moving away from the fingertip). The middle finger also helps to gently balance the stick in your hand. As you play, the stick may wiggle or toggle between the first and second knuckles slightly. However, never let it fall back into the web of your hand. When you use this grip, you will get a relaxed feel and a warmer, more resonant sound on your drums.

FIGURE 4-4:
Basic drum set patterns to get you started

Strike the snare drum with the left hand and the ride cymbal with the right hand.
(This assumes your drums are set up right handed.)

Chapter 5
Rock 101

This chapter introduces you to the nuts and bolts of rock drumming. The chapter begins with a brief discussion of rock drumming as an art form. Next, it outlines how to build stamina and endurance at loud volumes and how to reduce your risk of repetitive-motion injuries. You'll also find some basic rock beats here. These are practical "grooves" used by every drummer in all styles. While elementary, you will likely use these beats more than the more complex variations found later in the book.

5

Rock Drumming as Art

Too often, musicians trivialize rock drumming as if it's easy or simple. If you say, "I'm a rock drummer" to certain people, it may conjure up images of half-crazy hulks thrashing away at their monstrous kits. Even Jim Henson's character Animal, from the Muppets, helped further this stereotype.

Unfortunately, some drummers do help to perpetuate negative labeling. However, the vast majority of drummers are smart, multitalented, and thoughtful musicians. Certainly, drummers such as Neil Peart (Rush) and Bill Bruford (Yes, King Crimson) have done a lot to dispel the myth that drummers are simpletons or nonmusicians. Their professor-like intellectualism has been infectious, and this is reflected in their sophisticated playing. You too can help the cause, and the collective reputation of drummers, by treating rock drumming as an art form, not just another excuse to go bonkers on your drum kit.

Many prejudices about drummers have been dispelled, but even today you might hear a quartet described as "Three musicians and a drummer." Historically, drummers have often been portrayed as outsiders because they do not play a pitched instrument. It's your job to help change these perceptions.

How can you boost positive images of drumming?

- Treat your drums like an instrument. The drum set is a bona fide instrument worthy of your respect and every musician's respect. Therefore, play on your drums; do not pound on your drums.
- When you play with a group, listen and interact with the other musicians. If you do this, you will be seen as a contributing member of the band. If, on the other hand, you're self-involved, care only about playing "hot licks," and you play mind-numbingly loud, you may be seen as an insensitive musician. Yes, even in rock! From there, it's not long before you get grouped in with the other mythic ogres of the drum set.

- Take piano lessons. You don't have to become the next Franz Liszt, but you should learn the basics. More than anything, the perception that drummers are not musicians comes from the very real fact that most drummers do not understand music theory. In order to interact well with other musicians, you need to be able to talk the talk.

Outside of drumming, no one cares about paradiddles or buzz rolls. Most musicians are concerned with chords, melodies, and other harmonic elements. If you understand music theory, you will become a more acute listener. This, in turn, means that you will become a better accompanist. As a rock or pop drummer, your number one job will be to complement singers and soloists.

Playing with Power and Volume

In rock music, you must be able to accommodate many different stylistic milieus. As you know from Chapter 1, rock has many subgenres, and increasingly, these styles are being combined and recombined in unique ways. This means being able to play at all volumes. However, generally speaking, rock drummers are asked to play loud to very loud.

At first, playing loudly may seem easy. However, it's harder than it seems.

Loud playing is not easy because you must play consistently loud. Anyone can make inconsistent loud noises at the drum set. On the other hand, to play consistently and uniformly at a loud volume, you must posses a great deal of stick control as well as unflinching stamina.

FACT

Playing the drums is a cardio workout. Therefore, you must always breathe regularly and steadily. Unfortunately, some drummers hold their breath when they concentrate and this interferes with their endurance levels. If you maintain stable and consistent breathing, you will have much greater stamina and your playing will improve.

The snare drum and the bass drum provide the backbeat; therefore, they must be machine-like. Listen to the top rock drummers today and you will hear very consistent backbeats. For example, if the snare pattern on beats two and four (See Figure 5-1) varies dynamically, your playing will sound shaky and insecure. Similarly, if the bass drum rhythm on beats one and three contains erratic dynamics, your playing will sound timid and unsure. Rock beats can, and often do, incorporate ghost notes (see Chapter 9), but these must not interfere with steady and consistent snare- and kick-drum backbeats. In other words, when playing a backbeat, each snare crack and bass drum thud must be identical and strong. (This is the opposite of jazz, which favors multiple dynamic layers in the snare and bass drum.)

The same is true of the tom-toms when playing fills or incorporating them into beats. Often, you will want to move from drum to drum in a perfectly balanced, monodynamic fashion. Where appropriate, you may experiment with accents and ghost notes, but these must not interfere with your central musical (rhythmical) idea. In rock, fills must be powerful and sturdy; the ear must be able to instantly grab onto them and follow them to their logical conclusion.

How to Avoid Injury

Unfortunately, powerful playing has its costs. Tendonitis and carpel tunnel syndrome are common maladies in drumming. This is why you must play in the relaxed manner described in Chapter 3. But even if you play relaxed, the sheer force needed to play, night after night, in a rock setting can have a deleterious affects. Your hands, wrists, and arms could all be injured. Thankfully, some basic tips can help you play with all the power and volume you need, but without the extra muscle.

1. Set up your snare drum flat so you can strike the rim and the head at the same time when playing a backbeat. This is called a "rim shot." Rim shots vastly increase snare drum volume. When you use them, you can even save energy because you will get a big sound without much effort.

2. Tune your top snare drum head on the tighter side. Many drummers tune their snare drum too low. A taut snare drum head makes your playing

sound more articulated and crisp and you won't have to force the sound out of the drum as much. Overall, a snappy snare makes it easier for you to cut through the din of guitars and keyboards.

3. Use a single-ply top snare drum head. You must use a single-ply ultrathin head for the bottom of the snare drum. (Otherwise, the snare wires won't buzz.) However, some drummers use a double-ply head on the top of the snare to get a loud tone. The reverse is actually true: A thinner head allows the snare drum to project more clearly, cleanly, and articulately. Double-ply heads, like Remo's Pin Stripe, are better suited for tom-toms and bass drums.

4. Use a heavy ride cymbal and thin crashes. A heavy ride cymbal will allow you to cut through amplified instruments because you'll get a clear "ping" sound. On the ride, you want to avoid the dark, washy tones produced by thin cymbals. However, heavy crashes respond poorly and the tendency is to hit them too hard. Thinner crashes well up and shimmer instantly. The bottom line is that you will expend less energy and get better results with the appropriate cymbals.

5. Find the right drumsticks for *you*. Every drummer is different and, as stated earlier, playing situations vary too. Therefore, you should take time to experiment with many different models of sticks until you find the right one to suit your needs. In rock, you should look for a meatier stick. In other words, you'll want to choose one that has a thicker diameter, a longer shaft, and a substantial tip. Nylon tips add brightness to the cymbals, which is also a plus. When choosing sticks, avoid the gigantic models used by marching drummers (no "S" models). Also, look for sticks that have a gummy lacquer or finish. (Regal Tip products offer this on most models.) Sticks with a gummy lacquer allow you to hold the sticks looser in your hands. The less tension you have, the less your chance of injury.

6. Warm up before you play. You wouldn't run a marathon without first stretching and warming up your body. Likewise, don't jump on the bandstand cold. If you do, you're more likely to injure yourself. To avoid this, practice rudiments or other technical exercises at least fifteen

minutes before you go on stage. When doing so, start slowly then gradually increase the speed. There are also many stretching exercises you can perform. One very effective exercise involves placing the palm of your hand against a wall. Once you do this, *gently* pull back on your fingertips as you straighten your arm. This will flex your tendons and keep them from getting inflamed. Here's another quick tip: Run your hands under warm water just before you play. This is especially helpful if you're playing in a chilly environment.

Basic Rock Beats

It's time to learn some basic rock beats. The beats illustrated in Figures 5-1 and 5-2 use only three instruments: the hi-hat, the snare drum, and the bass drum. These are practical beats that you can use in many rock and pop contexts. In fact, listen for these beats and other variations when you next turn on the radio or attend a concert. The "grooves" outlined here are universal and ubiquitous. Every rock drummer knows them and uses them often.

The beat you see in Figure 5-1 is the basic rock groove. Most rock beats are based, one way or another, on this beat. In a sense, you could consider this beat to be the cornerstone of rock drumming. The most salient element here is the back-and-forth kick-snare, kick-snare rhythm. This pattern is often referred to as a backbeat. Figure 5-1 shows the bass drum playing on beats one and three and the snare drum playing on beats two and four. Tens of thousands of rock songs use this as its rhythmical backbone, even though variations may be used to spice up this pattern.

On all of the rock beats found in this chapter, and throughout this book, it's important to play each beat many times before moving on to the next example. A repeat symbol has been indicated at the end of each bar. Repeat each beat over and over in order to properly learn the pattern and internalize it.

FIGURE 5-1: Basic rock beat

Track 8

In Figure 5-2, you will see eight variations on the basic rock beat. These variations use quarter notes and eighth notes to alter the groove. It's important to note that only the bass drum has been altered. In beats one through four, you will see the snare drum maintained on beats two and four, while the bass drum plays variations. On beats five through eight, the backbeat is reversed. This means that the snare drum and bass drum are inverted, so the snare drum is on beats one and three and the bass drum plays variations on beats two and four. Beats five through eight are mostly used as "changeup" beats or clever alterations.

FIGURE 5-2: Basic rock variations

Track 9

Play each of these beats on loop!

Another pattern uses eight eighth notes on the bass drum together with snare hits on two and four, and in reverse, on one and three. This gives the music drive and forward momentum. These beats are best used as the music builds and climaxes. They are shown in Figure 5-3.

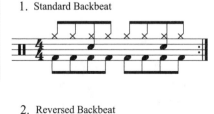

1. Standard Backbeat

2. Reversed Backbeat

Adding Eighth Rests

Now it is time to add eighth rests to the mix. You will still only alter the bass drum on these patterns; the snare drum will remain fixed on beats two and four. However, eighth rests are used to spice up the basic groove. This is illustrated in Figure 5-4, where you will see sixteen variations.

Remember that eighth rests are worth one-half a beat in 4/4 time. In Figure 5-4, the eighth rest appears only on downbeats. If they were to appear on an upbeat or "and," you would really be playing quarter notes in disguise. Why? In the world of drumming, an eighth note followed by an eighth rest is tantamount to a quarter note. This is because drums do not have controlled sustain.

A violinist or a trumpeter, for example, can sustain a note or cut it short. Therefore, they can play quarter notes differently from the eighth note-eighth rest pattern discussed above. The only way a drummer can sustain a note is through a roll. Buzz rolls best mimic the sustain of other instruments by creating a smooth "zzzzz" sound.

There are really many ways to play Figure 5-4. These are generic beats, but they are also extremely practical. Rock drummers use them (and others

FIGURE 5-4: Rock beats using eighth notes and eighth rests

Track 10

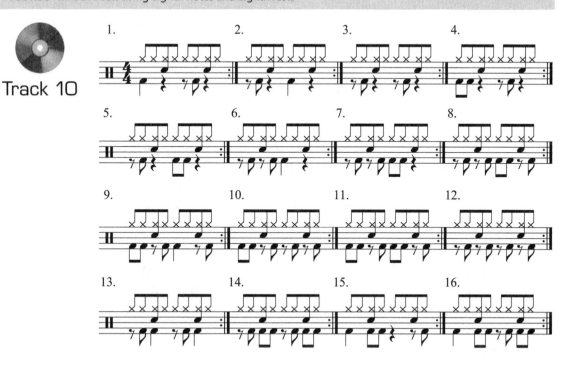

like them) all the time. That said, you should be able to get a lot of mileage out of these patterns. You can play these beats fast, slow, loud, or soft. You can also ride on the cymbal instead of the hi-hat. If you do, add the hi-hat foot on the downbeats of two and four (with the snare drum). If you're more advanced, you may also spruce these beats up by adding open and closed hi-hats (See Chapter 6) or accents and ghost notes (See Chapter 7).

Riding on the Cymbal

If you haven't tried riding on the cymbal yet, it's time to give it your best shot. For some, riding on the cymbal is a little harder than riding on the hi-hat, but if you're patient, you will get the hang of it in no time. Figure 5-5 features twelve beats that use the ride cymbal and the hi-hat foot. These grooves are similar, and in some cases, identical to beats you've seen previously. The big difference is the placement of the hi-hat foot on beats two and four in tandem with the snare drum.

When playing the hi-hat foot, keep your heel firmly planted on the footboard. This will put you in position to use the ankle-heel technique as described in Chapter 4. You want to get a strong "chick" sound when playing these beats. Therefore, you will need to clamp the cymbals together tightly in order to play each note.

Additionally, make sure your bottom hi-hat cymbal is slightly angled so you get a good "chick" sound. If your hi-hat cymbals align perfectly, a muted sound is produced. In order to get a good "chick," you need to vent the air. Some newer cymbals have holes drilled in the bottom hi-hat. Others have crimped edges so the air can escape. If you don't own these types of cymbals, don't despair. On virtually every hi-hat stand, a small, round knob or screw is found under the cymbals; it screws into the seat cup that holds the bottom cymbal. When you turn this knob, the felt pad and washer, located just under the cymbal, tilt. This allows the cymbals to clamp together in an uneven, slanted fashion. As a result, when you push down on the pedal, air is released and you get a strong "chick" sound. As you play, the "chick" should complement the "ping" of the ride cymbal.

FIGURE 5-5:
Rock beats using the ride cymbal and hi-hat foot

Meg White is a self-taught rock drummer who has propelled the unique alternative rock duo The White Stripes since 1997. Using basic rock grooves like the ones detailed in this chapter, White has proven that less is more, most of the time. If you're not careful, multifaceted, "busy" beats can cloud a song. Listen to White's solid drumming on the albums *Elephant* and *Icky Thump*.

Before you ride on your cymbal, you should know a little bit more about cymbals. Every cymbal contains the following elements: a center hole, a bow, and an edge. Unless you're using a flat ride, your cymbals will also have a bell. The center hole allows the cymbal to be suspended. The bell is the raised cup found in the middle of the cymbal. The bow is the curved area or main body of the cymbal. It is found between the bell and the edge.

When riding on the cymbal, you will want to play on the bow of the cymbal. You can ride on the bell and the edge of the cymbal, but you should first learn how to get a good sound on the bow. You'll notice that the timbre or tone color of the cymbal changes drastically as you move from the edge to the bell. Where in the bow should you strike? Play in the middle of the timbral spectrum, between the darker tones of the edge and the brighter tones of the bell.

Chapter 6

Intermediate Rock Grooves

At this point, you know how to play rock grooves with bass drum variations. This chapter includes snare drum embellishments and more complex rhythms. To make sure you're ready to move on, play each beat from Chapter 5 with a metronome. This is the litmus test for any groove, fill, or solo. If you're having a difficult time with the metronome, slow the tempo down. Move on to this next group of beats only after you've mastered the material in the previous chapters. Remember, Chapters 2—11 in this book are cumulative.

Snare Drum Embellishments

The beats illustrated in Figure 6-1 use eighth notes and eighth rests to spice up the snare drum. In this figure, the bass drum remains fixed on beats one and three (except number eighteen). Later, you will combine snare and bass drum variations, but for now, you should focus on crisp, articulate snare drumming. You will notice that most of these patterns still retain a strong backbeat. This means that, despite any embellishments, the downbeats of two and four are often preserved. On the examples that stray from two-and-four downbeats, you will see upbeats used. This is a classic example of rhythmic displacement. This means that the snare will play on the upbeats or "+."

The beats in this chapter may also be played riding on the cymbal. When you do this, add the hi-hat foot on the downbeats of two and four. Be careful to keep the hi-hat consistent, especially as the snare drum varies; the tendency will be to change the hi-hat foot along with the snare drum.

Some patterns in Figure 6-1 displace the snare drum one eighth note to the left. This means that you will strike the snare drum on the "+" of one and/or the "+" of three. When you use both variations at once, you totally obfuscate the downbeats on two and four. (See #9 for a clear example of this.) In this case, you have a beat best used as a beat-fill combination. This concept is explained in Chapter 9. Lastly, you may play the snare drum on all four downbeats. For instance, the standard Motown beat incorporates downbeats on one, two, three, and four.

Beats #17 and #18 from Figure 6-1 show you some basic Motown grooves. The bass drum pattern is altered to all downbeats on example #18. This is commonly called four on the floor. You first saw this bass drum rhythm on beat #1 in Figure 5-2.

FACT

Motown is a regional style of rhythm and blues (R&B) that flourished in the 1960s. It featured such artists as The Marvelettes, The Supremes, Martha & The Vandellas, Smokey Robinson, and many more. Motown was born in Detroit, Michigan, and its full name, Motor Town, derives from Detroit's status as the automobile capital of the United States.

FIGURE 6-1: Snare drum variations

Track 11

Using Sixteenth Notes and Rests

Now that you've learned how to use quarter notes, eighth notes, and eighth rests to build rock beats, it's time to move on to sixteenth notes. As you know, if you take a quarter note and divide it into four equal parts, you have sixteenth notes. A better way to conceive of this is: four sixteenth notes equal one beat.

The question always comes up with students, "Aren't sixteenth notes *really* fast?" The answer is yes and no. Rhythms are not necessarily fast. The tempo you choose dictates how fast or slow a rhythm is played. If you play sixteenth notes at two hundred beats per minute, you will be playing fast. However, if you play sixteenth notes at seventy-five beats per minute, they become much more manageable.

This is an important concept to understand because when you practice the rock patterns in Figure 6-3, you will want to go slowly at first. If you try to play them blistering fast right off the bat, you're likely to fall short. In truth, slow, steady, accurate playing is the key to fast playing; when you learn a pattern at a slow speed, you set the stage for faster interpretations.

Before you play the rock patterns in Figure 6-3, look at how the hi-hat relates to an eighth-two sixteenth rhythmic combination. As you play Figure 6-2, say to yourself "together, together, bass." This rhythm is counted one–and–ah. The third note ("ah" or "bass") should not contain a hi-hat note. Most students add a hi-hat by mistake, so be very careful in your rendering of this rhythm. To fully understand what is being explained here, you must refer to Figure 6-2.

Figure 6-3 contains rock patterns that use sixteenth notes in the bass drum. For these beats, snare drum embellishments have been avoided. Instead, the snare drum only plays downbeats on two and four.

FIGURE 6-2:
Hi-hat and bass drum interaction

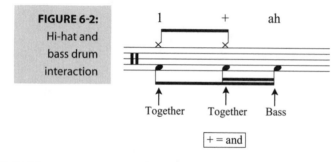

FIGURE 6-3: Using sixteenth notes in the bass drum

Track 12

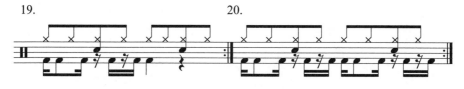

Pattern #'s 1, 9, 13, and 22 are played on the CD.

Figure 6-3 begins with eighth-two sixteenth rhythmic combinations. As you progress, you will see the reverse: a two sixteenth-eighth rhythm. The former is easier to play because there is a break between the eighth note and two sixteenths; the latter is more difficult to play because the rhythmical break occurs after you play the three notes. (This concept will become much more clear after you play the rhythm.) In short, you will probably need to slow the tempo down when you first play examples 9 and 10.

In Figure 6-3 you will also see patterns that focus on +-ah as well as dotted eighth-sixteenth rhythms. Additionally, you will see patterns that use sixteenth-eighth-sixteenth combinations. Finally, you will see patterns that use a lone "e" and "ah" in conjunction with quarter notes and downbeats. Beat #17 and beat #18 use single sixteenth notes without any downbeat resolution; this creates an angular yet funky feel to the groove.

There are many bass drum variations that can be formed using quarter notes, eighth notes, sixteenth notes, quarter rests, eighth rests, and sixteenth rests. Figure 6-3 only shows you a handful of them; therefore, you should experiment with your own patterns. Can you use the rhythms you've learned so far to write some of your own rock beats? Figure 6-4 gives you four opportunities to do this. You may want to use your own staff paper to write out even more!

FIGURE 6-4:
Writing your
own rock beats

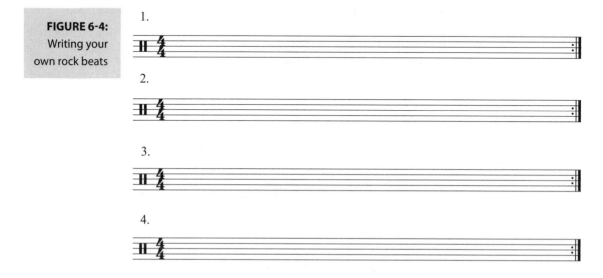

Use quarter notes, eighth notes, sixteenth notes, and rests to write your own beats!

Beginner Snare and Bass Drum Combinations

Snare and bass drum combinations are the next logical step in playing rock variations. The first set of beats, shown in Figure 6-5, use only quarter notes, quarter rests, eighth notes, and eighth rests (no sixteenths). Some of these beats move very far away from the basic rock groove you learned in Figure 5-1.

For example, beat #15 in Figure 6-5 offsets the bass drum and snare drum groove by one eighth note. Furthermore, both the kick and snare are displaced equally. Because of this, it's easy to get confused and lose track of where you are in the measure. In other words, you might forget where beat one is. To avoid flipping the rhythm around in your head, count diligently.

Beat #11 creates a double-time feel. Double time simply means that you are playing double the speed. In #11, the speed and time signature have not technically changed. However, it feels like double time because the snare drum plays on all upbeats.

Beat #11 could be written in 2/2 or cut time. If you write it in 2/2, the beat will technically become double time. In this meter, the half note equals one beat, not the quarter note; this means that the pulse is measured in half notes. If you were to write beat #11 in 2/2 time, the bass drum, snare drum, and hi-hat would all be written using quarter notes. What does this really mean? Quarter notes in 2/2 function the same way as eighth notes in 4/4.

Beat #16 from Figure 6-5 emulates a single paradiddle (see Chapter 3). A single paradiddle contains the sticking: right, left, right, right, left, right, left, left. In beat #16, this same concept is used. Here, the beat is broken up between the left hand (snare drum) and the right foot (bass drum). Specifically, the bass drum acts as the right hand and the pattern bass, snare, bass, bass, snare, bass, snare, snare is created. This toggling back and forth mimics the sound and feel of the single paradiddle and you should feel free to stretch the definition of the single paradiddle to include such applications.

FIGURE 6-5: Beginner snare and bass drum combinations

Track 13

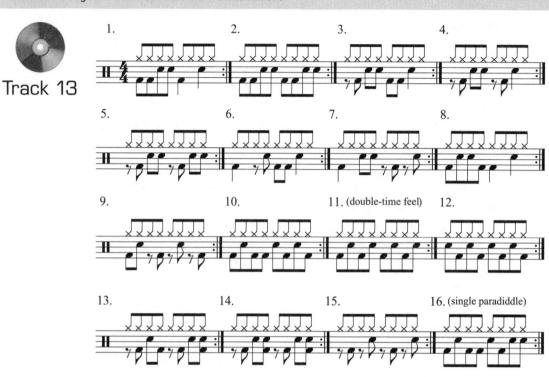

1.   2.   3.   4.

5.   6.   7.   8.

9.   10.   11. (double-time feel)   12.

13.   14.   15.   16. (single paradiddle)

Pattern #'s 1, 7, and 16 are played on the CD.

Intermediate Snare and Bass Drum Combinations

Like Figure 6-5, the beats in Figure 6-6 use snare and bass drum combinations. However, here you will see sixteenth notes and sixteenth rests added to the mix. Although these beats are still considered intermediate by professionals, some of them get quite tricky. Additionally, some of these beats can sound "busy" in real musical contexts. This is where taste and appropriateness come into play.

In Figure 6-6 you will see some of the patterns that can be made using quarter notes, eighth notes, and sixteenth notes. If you shift the order of the notes or experiment with different rhythmical combinations, you can create many more permutations. Like the examples shown in Figures 6-1, 6-3, and 6-5, this figure is merely a sampling of the kinds of beats that can be developed through rhythmic combinations.

How do you develop taste and appropriateness? Listen to music as much as possible. Get a sense for how drummers approach each style of rock. Playing experience is also an invaluable teacher. Through trial and error, success and failure, you will eventually develop the ability to know when you're overplaying, when you're underplaying, or when you're right on!

Figure 6-6 begins with eighth-two sixteenth combinations. You should remember this rhythm from Figure 6-3 and from reading etudes in Chapter 2. These rhythmic combos are placed in both the bass drum and the snare. Figure 6-6 continues with dotted eighth–sixteenth variations. As you progress, you will see the two sixteenth-eighth pattern. Next, some eighth and sixteenth rests are added; these spice up beats 9–11. This is followed by a return to eighth-two sixteenth combinations and other familiar rhythms. Only this time, these rhythms are broken up between the kick and snare in new ways. For example, in beats 12–16, you will see the snare and bass drum alternate back and forth using eighth-two sixteenth rhythms.

Figure 6-6 ends with single paradiddle patterns and inverted single paradiddle patterns. Paradiddles can be inverted a number of ways. Here, the "diddle" comes before the "para." This means that the double sticking precedes the single sticking. For beats 20 and 21, the bass drum assumes the role of the right hand as it plays doubles or "diddles."

FIGURE 6-6: Intermediate snare and bass drum combinations

Track 14

* = single paradiddle between the bass drum and the snare

* * = inverted single paradiddle between the bass drum and the snare

Pattern #'s 1, 10, 19, and 21 are played on the CD.

Using an Open Hi-Hat

When you open the hi-hat, you add yet another dimension to rock beats. In Figures 6–8, you will see "o" and "+." The "o" tells you to open the hi-hat cymbals. This means to release the pedal. When you do this, the cymbals will ring when you strike them.

There are varying degrees of open, and you should experiment with different sounds when playing Figure 6-7. In other words, use this as an opportunity to explore the rich colors inherent in your hi-hat cymbals. Too often, drummers only use one sound for open hi-hats. However, different sounds can be created depending on how much you release the cymbals with your foot.

A half-open sound is created by slightly loosening up on the hi-hat pedal. This creates a washy tone, which you will explore further in later chapters. If you release the pedal all the way, you will hear only the top cymbal resonate as you play open hi-hats. If you release the pedal mostly, but still keep the cymbals close enough together to touch when wiggled, another washy, yet meatier, tone will be produced.

Where you strike the cymbals also affects the sound(s) you make. For a thin sound, play on top of the cymbal. For an even thinner tone, ride on the bell. For a chunky sound, use the shaft of the stick to play on the edge of the cymbals. Other gradients can be created as well. See what other timbres you can generate.

In Figure 6-7, the open hi-hat sounds occur on the upbeats of beats 1–5. The open hi-hats are then transferred to downbeats on examples 6–9. Beats 10–16 use the bass drum variations first shown to you in Figure 5-2. Why the parenthesis in beats 2, 5, and 10–13? The first time through each beat, the hi-hat is already closed. Therefore, parenthetical plus signs (+) are indicated to remind you to close the hi-hat on each repeat.

Figure 6-8 contains nine intermediate open hi-hat patterns. Here, you will see sixteenth notes used in both the snare and the bass drum. Again, these are beats you have already seen. These are all taken from Figure 6-3. However, now open hi-hats have been added on both upbeats and downbeats.

FIGURE 6-7: Open hi-hat patterns

Track 15

Pattern #'s 1, 11, and 15 are played on the CD.

FIGURE 6-8: Intermediate open hi-hat patterns

Track 16

1.
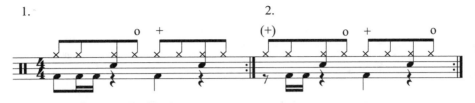

3.
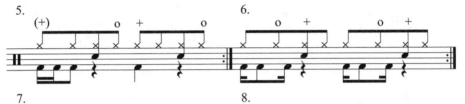

5.

7.

9.

Pattern #'s 1, 6, and 9 are played on the CD.

FIGURE 6-9: Drum Set Etude #1

Track 17

FIGURE 6-10: Drum Set Etude #2

Track 18

Drum Set Etudes #1 and #2

Drum Set Etudes #1 and #2 bring together all of the rhythmical patterns you've learned so far. Additionally, some new rhythmical groupings are found here. However, no new rhythms are included here. This means that you will only see quarter, eighth, and sixteenth notes in these study pieces (and corresponding rests).

In the previous drum set figures, you only played one-bar phrases. In Figures 6-9 and 6-10, you're asked to play twelve-bar phrases. This is quite a disparity. The best way to learn each etude is in steps. But where do you begin?

First, practice each measure individually. In other words, practice each measure on loop until you feel comfortable with it. After this, start grouping them together. Begin by playing two-measure phrases. Once you're comfortable with this, try playing a full line (three measures). After this, group two lines together (six measures). Lastly, read all three lines (twelve measures). You may also work in two-, four-, six-, eight-, ten-, and twelve-bar phrases if you choose.

By learning music in chunks or fragments, your job becomes much more manageable. On the other hand, if you try to play from beginning to end and never take the time to concentrate on the individual measures, you may run into roadblocks. Occasionally, you may even need to break each pattern down into individual beats or pulses. This was done in Figure 6-2 where you saw only one-and-ah. This is okay, too!

No matter how you approach the following etudes, be sure to practice them in time. You may play slowly, but you must keep a steady pulse. Use a metronome to ensure proper timekeeping. If you practice out of time, you will play out of time in a real playing situation. Indeed, you are what you practice.

FIGURE 6-11:
Hi-hat foot
ostinatos

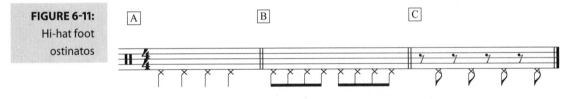

Try these hi-hat foot ostinatos with Figures 6-9 and 6-10!

Hi-Hat Foot Ostinatos

Etudes #1 and #2 in Figures 6-9 and 6-10 use only hi-hat, snare, and bass drum. As written, the hi-hat is your ride surface. However, you can play these etudes many different ways. One way is to switch your ride surface to the cymbal. Once you do this, a variety of hi-hat foot ostinatos come into play.

FACT

An ostinato is a rhythmic or melodic pattern that is repeated on loop. Ostinatos remain fixed or unchanging. In other words, they do not evolve or vary in any way. However, other patterns or themes are usually layered over ostinatos; this may include additional ostinatos. Drummers use ostinatos regularly in rock and other styles of music.

The hi-hat ostinatos presented in Figure 6-11 are among the most common and effective in rock. Use these ostinatos on Drum Set Etude #1 and Drum Set Etude #2 (Figures 6-9 and 6-10). You can also use these patterns on just about any rock beat, including any of the grooves you learned earlier in the chapter. Remember, in order to use these ostinatos, you must switch your ride surface to the cymbal. Also, any open hi-hat indications will be omitted.

In terms of technique, you may use either the heel's-up position, where you dance on the ball of your foot, or the heel's-down position, where you play from the ankle. When you use the latter, your hi-hat ostinatos will not be as prominent or loud. On the upside, you may feel more comfortable as you sit at the kit. (Sometimes lifting your heels throws off your balance.)

See Chapter 4 for descriptions of the heel's-down and heel's-up positions. They are explained in relationship to the bass drum; however, these techniques have full application on the hi-hat as well.

Chapter 7

Sophisticated Rock Grooves

In this chapter, you will learn how to apply accents to beats. You will also learn about ghost notes and explore triplets on the drum set. Specifically, you will have a chance to play beats using sixteenth-note triplets. This will be followed by two etudes that combine eighth and sixteenth notes—plus corresponding rests—with triplets, accents, buzzes, and ghost notes. Through these etudes, you will get a chance to synthesize the material you've been honing in the last three chapters.

Accents, Ghost Notes, and Buzz Strokes

Novice drummers usually don't realize how important it is to build color and depth into a drumbeat. However, this sensibility (and skill) separates the amateur from the pro. In order to rise above mechanical "bookish" playing, you must create dynamic layers in your beats. If your drumbeats are monodynamic, they may sound stiff and plain. Dynamics bring tension and release to music and they make music sound much more natural and flowing. The best way to do this is by using accents and ghost notes.

You were introduced to accents in Chapter 3. As you know, an accent is a sudden emphasis in the music. Figure 7-1 features beats that use accents in the hi-hat. In Chapter 11, you will learn how to use different ride ostinatos. The accented beats found here should serve as an introduction to these more advanced hi-hat applications. When you play the grooves in Figure 7-1, be sure to show a sharp contrast between the accented notes and the unaccented notes. In Chapter 9, you will learn about accents in greater detail as you learn how to play intermediate- to advanced-level snare drum fills.

FIGURE 7-1: Rock beats with hi-hat accents

Ghost notes are a critical part of any style of drumming. In rock, they make your beats sound rich with nuance and rhythmical inflection. Ghost notes are the opposite of accents. In fact, you could think of them as the "anti-accent." An accent is a sudden emphasis; a ghost note is a very soft tap. These taps are called ghost notes because they are so quiet, the ear only barely perceives of them. Figure 7-2 shows you twelve beats that use ghost notes. The ghost notes are indicated in parenthesis and they are found only

FIGURE 7-2: Rock beats with ghost notes

Track 19

Pattern #'s 1, 5, and 11 are played on the CD.

in the snare drum (left hand). Be sure to play them extremely soft; listen to the accompanying CD to hear how they should sound.

Another common technique used by pros is the buzz stroke. Buzz rolls are commonly used in fills and solos. However, some drummers forget how effective buzz strokes can be when used in beats.

In Figure 7-3, you will see buzz strokes implemented in the snare drum. The buzzes are indicated with a "z." Unlike their use in rolls, the buzzes found here only use one buzz stroke at a time. As you know, the buzz roll uses a series of tightly woven buzzes to create a beautiful "zzzzzz" sound. In this context, these single buzzes add color and texture to the beat.

Except for numbers 9 and 10, the buzz is paired up with a bass drum hit in each example of Figure 7-3. In these cases, it acts as a pick-up note. Ultimately, the buzz ornaments the bass drum. If you need to review how to play a buzz, see Chapter 3. Remember to use Fulcrum #1 so that you

FIGURE 7-3: Rock beats with buzz strokes

Track 20

Pattern #'s 1, 5, and 12 are played on the CD.

can create a smooth, articulate sound. When buzzing on the downbeats in example numbers 7–10, allow the stick to buzz for the full duration of the beat. In other words, don't choke the buzz too quickly.

Sixteenth-Note Triplets in the Snare Drum

Like buzzes, triplets in the snare drum are often used to ornament a bass drum pattern. In Figure 7-4, you will notice that only the second and third triplets in a three-note group are used. This is commonplace in rock drumming.

In order to play the two aforementioned triplet notes articulately, you will need to rely on your double-stroke roll technique. If your kit is set up righty, the two-note triplet pattern will be played "LL." You will want to snap the stick with your wrist for the first or primary stroke and let the stick bounce for the second or secondary stroke. After you allow the bounce on the secondary stroke, use your fingers—middle, ring, and pinky—to gently squeeze the stick. This will stop it from bouncing a third time. All of this assumes you're using matched grip.

When two triplets in the snare precede a bass drum note, the pattern suggests a three-stroke ruff. In this case, the ruff is broken up between a "LL" snare sticking and a bass drum. In order to create a ruff sound, you will need to play the patterns in Figure 7-4 at medium to fast speeds.

Triplets create a rolling or undulating feel in music. This is especially true when you fill up each measure with a large quantity of triplets. In example 8 from Figure 7-4, you will see sixteen triplets used in the left hand. However, if you include the bass drum hits and the two right-handed downbeats (on beats two and four), twenty-four triplets are ultimately created. This is a full measure of sixteenth-note triplets. Each beat contains six triplets and six triplets × four beats = twenty-four triplets.

This type of ornamentation brings up another hairy issue: a shift in the hi-hat part. In Figure 7-4, example numbers 6–8 are the first beats in this text to use an altered hi-hat. So far, you've only seen straight eighth notes. However, when you play these beats, you must cross your right hand over the left to play select downbeats.

ALERT!

Beat numbers 6–8 in Figure 7-4 are designed to go very fast. If you can play them at around 120 beats per minute (BPM), the rhythm will start to sound like a one-handed roll. However, don't try to play fast right off the bat. When practicing these, and all triplet patterns, go slowly at first and pick up the tempo gradually.

In pattern number 6, you will cross the right hand over the left hand on the downbeat of two. For beats 7 and 8, your right hand will cross over the left hand on the downbeats of two and four. When you do this, the hi-hat must be omitted, but it is not missed. Given the amount of rhythmical activity, the absent hi-hat notes are not even noticed. To cross your hand, simply arc your arm over the left (snare) hand.

FIGURE 7-4: Sixteenth-note triplets in the snare drum

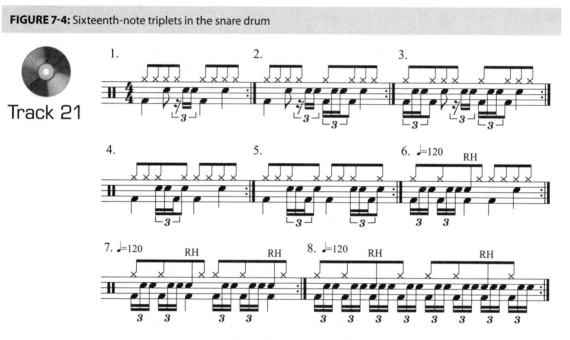

Track 21

Pattern #'s 1, 5, and 8 are played on the CD.

Sixteenth-Note Triplets in the Bass Drum

Sixteenth-note triplets in the bass drum are very effective in rock, and you will hear players such as John Bonham (Led Zeppelin) and Ginger Baker (Cream) use them as well as new generations of drummers including Abe Laboriel Jr. (independent), Carter Beauford (Dave Mathews Band), and many more. Despite the wide range of applications, sixteenth-note triplets cannot be played on the kick drum at extremely fast tempos unless you use a double pedal. (See Chapters 13 and 14.)

Like the snare drum triplets illustrated in Figure 7-4, the bass patterns in Figure 7-5 use only the second and third notes in a three-note triplet pattern. You could play all three triplets, but the tempo would have to be rather slow or you would need to use a double pedal.

There are two bass drum techniques you can use in Figure 7-5. If you remember from Chapter 4, you learned about the ankle-heel or heel's-down technique. You also learned about the heel's up-foot slide approach.

If you're playing at a softer dynamic, you should use the heel's-down technique on the beats found in Figure 7-5. However, the heel's up-foot slide is ideal for rock settings where you are required to play at a loud volume. When you use this technique, the ball of your foot should be positioned in the middle of the pedal footboard for the first note. After you push down the pedal, you will then slide into the second note. Your foot should land at the top of the pedal as the second note is produced. After this, you will need to bring your foot back into position—in the middle of the footboard—in preparation for another pair of triplets.

FIGURE 7-5: Sixteenth-note triplets in the bass drum

Track 22

Pattern #'s 1 and 6 are played on the CD.

Snare Drum and Bass Drum Triplet Combinations

Building snare and bass drum triplet combinations is particularly fun, albeit challenging. In Figure 7-6, you will see some examples of how triplets can be placed in both the snare hand and the bass drum. If you have a double pedal, do not cheat! These patterns are to be played with one pedal. The only exception to this would be if you wanted to play these beats at extremely fast tempos (above 132 beats per minute).

Despite the fact that there is a lot of rhythmical activity going on here, most of these examples still feature a standard two-and-four snare drum backbeat. It may be hidden in the mix, but it's there! Exceptions to this include number 3. Here you are asked to play all four quarter notes in the snare as the bass drum interjects triplets.

The busier any beat gets the less practical it becomes in a real-life context. In truth, most rock drummers find themselves playing basic grooves similar to the ones presented in Chapter 5. However, all the fancy rhythms you've been learning do have their place and they are necessary for your development.

For example, the beats in figure 7-6 can be used to spruce up the end of a phrase in a song. They may also be used to add a colorful rhythmical diversion or interlude. This is especially true of example numbers 9 and 10. These specific beats are derived from the double-stroke roll. Here, you will see two bass-drum notes combined with two snare drum strokes. Like earlier examples, which borrowed from the single paradiddle, this pattern emulates a rudiment. (You'll find this happens more and more in this book.) In this case, the right hand is swapped out or substituted with the right leg of the bass drum. Again, this assumes you're playing a right-handed setup.

FIGURE 7-6: Snare drum and bass drum triplet combinations

Track 23

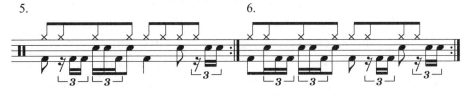

Pattern #'s 1, 6, and 10 are played on the CD.

Drum Set Etudes #3 and #4

The drum set etudes that comprise Figures 7-7 and 7-8 are both twelve measures long. They also include a cymbal crash on beat four of measure twelve. With the exception of open hi-hat techniques, everything you have learned in the last three chapters is employed here. You will see:

- Quarter notes
- Eighth notes
- Dotted eighth notes
- Eighth rests
- Sixteenth notes
- Sixteenth rests
- Sixteenth-note triplets
- Accents
- Ghost notes

Use the list above to review your strengths and weaknesses. As a burgeoning rock musician, you need to constantly assess and reassess your abilities. The only way to do this is through self-inquiry and constructive criticism. This means asking hard questions. For example, can you play steady sixteenth notes in the kick drum? Are you able to play clean buzzes using Fulcrum #1? Can you use both the heel's-up and heel's-down bass-drum techniques? How's that foot slide coming along?

If you're having a difficult time assessing your strengths and weaknesses, record your drumming and listen back. This will give you an opportunity to listen to your drumming from a distance or as a third party. It can be hard to tell what's going on—good or bad—when you're caught up in the mechanics of real-time performance.

In addition to this, reflect on the various rhythmical combinations you've been working with so far. For instance, the eighth-two sixteenth pattern has been used quite often in this book. So has the dotted eighth-sixteenth pattern. Additionally, you saw sixteenth-eighth-sixteenth combinations popping up over and over. Lastly, paradiddle and inverted paradiddle combinations—between the bass drum and snare drum—have been used recurrently. Study all of these rhythms meticulously; these are the staples of rock beats.

There are two general questions you should also ask yourself:

1. Are you playing in steady time? Rushing is more common than dragging. However, dragging can be a problem, especially if you find the music to be technically challenging. As previously stated, metronomes will help you develop a keen internal clock.
2. Are you interpreting each beat or playing mechanically?

When you play any beat in this book, you must think about feel. Feel is very difficult to teach and even harder to explain. Indeed, feel is a nebulous concept. If you play in perfect time, and render each rhythm exactly, you're on the right track. But this isn't everything. If your feel is lacking, you still might find yourself unable to get a gig. Therefore, don't underestimate its importance.

FIGURE 7-7: Drum Set Etude #3

Track 24

FIGURE 7-8: Drum Set Etude #4

Track 25

Playing with Feel

The best way to achieve a good feel is to listen to the kind of music you're trying to play. Most of the beats you've learned in this book can be applied to a wide variety of rock styles. For example, the etudes included in Figures 7-7 and 7-8 could be applied to both a hard rock and a funk setting. It all depends on how you interpret the notes.

To play Figures 7-7 and 7-8 in a hard rock style, you will want to hit very hard. This means using your arms and wrists to strike the drums and cymbals extremely loud. To do this, you'll want to create a flowing, wave-like movement in your arms and wrists. The eighth-note ride pattern you play on the hi-hat should also be played on the edge of the cymbals. This is how you will get a chunkier sound. Further, you will not want to clamp the hi-hat cymbals down tightly; instead, ease up on the pedal slightly so that you get a fatter sound.

You could even experiment with a half-open hi-hat sound if you wish. For this, see Chapter 12. On the snare, you will want to use rim shots except on ghost notes and buzz strokes. To enhance your hard rock feel, you should use a large kick drum (22" diameter or bigger) and slightly detune the snare drum so that you get a warm, punchy sound.

To play these beats using a funk feel, you will want to create a tight, crisp sound. To do this, you could use a piccolo snare since it has a shallower shell. You could also create a crisp tone by tuning your snare drum to a high pitch. In other words, you'll want the snare to have a taut, crackling sound. On bass drum, a big, meaty sound is optimal in modern funk so you would want to use a large-diameter drum.

Even though proper gear is essential, equipment alone cannot create feel. To play Figures 7-7 and 7-8 using a funky feel, clamp the hi-hat cymbals together very tightly so you get a clean, articulate sound—this will complement the crackle of your taut snare drum. Then, play each etude with intent, but don't feel the need to over blow. Funk does not rely on ear-splitting volume; it does rely on tight, snappy playing.

ESSENTIAL

One of the finest hard rock drummers in rock history was John Bonham of Led Zeppelin. Led Zeppelin I, II, and III are among their most legendary albums. James Brown's records are among the best funk examples in history. His drummers Melvin Parker, Clyde Stubblefield, and John "Jabo" Starks epitomized funk drumming in the 1960s and 1970s.

Ultimately, feel comes down to two seemingly unrelated components: how relaxed you are and how well you understand the style of music you're playing. No matter what genre(s) you're attempting, great feel is the result of relaxed playing and a thorough grasp of music history. This is why, in this book, you will continually be reminded to listen, listen, and listen some more.

FACT

Warm-ups are not just for your body. A proper warm-up routine will get your mind ready to think, concentrate, and react. For that reason, you should choose warm-ups that engage and invigorate both your limbs and your brain. Don't know where to start? Play Figures 3-7 and 3-8 as warm-ups.

To get a relaxed sound, warm up before you perform. There are many warm-ups espoused by drummers and teachers alike. As mentioned in Chapter 5, a warm-up is a technical exercise designed to get your hands and feet moving. Rudiments work well as warm-ups, so do the exercises found in the snare drum books listed in Appendix A. The important thing to remember when warming up is to go slowly at first. Start at a comfortable speed then gradually increase the tempo as the blood gets flowing. If you feel stiff during your warm-up, reduce the tempo; never push yourself over the edge when warming up.

Chapter 8
Filling Around the Kit

Drum set playing consists primarily of beats and fills. In this chapter, you will focus strictly on fills. The first group of fills found here will be played on the snare drum. Then you will learn how to orchestrate fills around a five-piece drum kit. After this, you will play fills that incorporate the bass drum. Then, you will learn how to use rolls to fill. Finally, you will add flams, three-stroke ruffs, and double-stops. All this will serve as a primer for developing your own professional-sounding fills.

Drum Fills 101

A lot of drummers have "chops." This is slang for great technique, facility, or if you want to be literal, mechanical skill. The problem with many drummers is that they don't know how to implement their chops. When it comes to fills, these inadequacies can become glaring. For example, some drummers don't know when to fill. Consequently, they fill too much and in the wrong spots. This makes the music sound busy and cluttered. Properly placed fills are essential. Therefore, it's best to live by this rule: If you don't know where to play a fill, don't play one.

A fill should be a bridge between two phrases or sections in a song. On occasion, it might also serve as an "answer" to a musical "question" as posed by a soloist. Question and answer solos are more prevalent in jazz, however. In rock and pop, your job is to find the holes in the music and to literally fill them up with sound so the song feels seamless and polished.

Each phrase and or section of a song must tie together neatly. At its simplest, a fill might consist of a cymbal crash. At its most complex, a fill might feature whipping tom-tom licks around the kit. It all depends on the requirements and style of the song. For instance, a Jimi Hendrix song will allow for lots of freewheeling fills. On the other hand, an Avril Lavigne pop tune will be less jam oriented. Fills may be as short as a half a beat or they may be as long as four measures; the latter is less common. Anything beyond four bars should really be considered a solo.

Listen to the drummers documented in Appendix A. These guys and gals represent some of the finest rock players ever. Get a sense for where they fill and what kind of fill they create. You'll find, more often than not, that fills help to outline the structure of a song. They transition the listener from verse to chorus, bridges to guitar solo, etc.

Fills purposely break up or interrupt beats. There are many ways to play fills and there are thousands of permutations available, but before you begin playing any fill, you must remember that fills have to be played in time. Most musical train wrecks occur on the bandstand when a drummer loses the time during a fill. When this happens, drummers often drop beats.

For example, rather than playing a fill in 4/4, the drummer might play three beats (3/4) by mistake. When this happens, the underpinning of the music gets tangled up and the band might fall apart. Consequently, you must take great care when filling. If you're a beginner, make sure you count each beat in the measure. Also, like beats, make sure you don't rush or drag when you fill.

Simple Fills on the Snare Drum

To start learning about fills, practice playing fills on the snare drum. The snare drum has more drive and crack than any other drum on your kit, so snare fills should be used when you want to give a song extra oomph or a boost of energy. In this case, rim shots—hitting the head and rim simultaneously—help to add forward momentum and excitement to your fill.

FACT

This chapter focuses mostly on full-measure fills. While these may be the most common type of fills for beginners, half-beat, one-beat, and three-beat fills are also very effective. Be sure to borrow segments from licks in this chapter to create fills of varying lengths. Be careful not to drop or add beats to the measure as you do this.

The most basic snare drum fill is one measure of eighth notes. (Unless the tempo is really fast, plain quarter notes are usually too simple or plain.) Figure 8-1 shows you a one-measure fill preceded by three measures of a basic beat. All totaled, you will be playing a four-bar phrase. Four-measure phrases are extremely common in rock and popular music, as are multiples of four, particularly eights and sixteens. As previously stated, it's important to think about phrases when you fill because your job is to glue together each section in the song.

For extra limb control and independence, practice playing the hi-hat foot on the downbeats of two and four as you play each fill. This will be difficult at first. However, if you can do this successfully, you will be well on your way toward developing four-way coordination.

In Figure 8-1, you will see a cymbal crash on beat one of the first measure. You will not play this crash when you first begin the pattern; you will only crash on the repeat. In real music, crashes are common, but not essential, after each fill. If you do crash, always play a bass drum or a snare drum with the crash. Naked crashes lack proper punch and your fill will lack closure.

FIGURE 8-1:
Eighth-note fill on the snare drum

This is a four-measure phrase!

As stated earlier, there's no rule stating that fills must be one full measure. They can be longer or shorter in varying degrees. Figure 8-2 shows you Figure 8-1 broken in half. In other words, it is truncated so you will play the fill on beats three and four only. As before, a crash is indicated on beat one of the first measure. Play the crash on the repeat only.

Next, in Figure 8-3, you will find a set of one-measure snare drum fills. These fills use quarter notes, eighth notes, sixteenth notes, and occasionally rests. Later, you will play more complex and meaty fills. For now, however, learn these straight, no-nonsense licks. These are practical and easy to pull off in a live context. Often, you'll find that simpler fills complement the music more than complex ones anyway!

FIGURE 8-2:
Half-measure
fill on the
snare drum

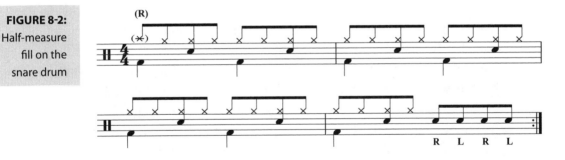

Like before, pair these fills up with a basic rock beat (See Figure 8-1) in a four-bar phrase. Also, begin each fill with the right hand and end with the left hand. In between, you may use a combination of double and single strokes as you wish.

FIGURE 8-3:
Snare drum
fill variations

Fills Using the Snare and Tom-Toms

The next batch of fills uses the snare drum and the tom-toms. These are written for a standard five-piece drum set, which includes three tom-toms (two racks and one floor). The first fill is a very common clockwise movement around the kit moving from the snare to the high-rack tom to the middle-rack tom and to the floor tom. The second fill does the exact reverse. Keep in mind that you do not have to use all three tom-toms in every fill.

Like the snare drum fills, you should play a basic rock beat for three measures, then play the fill. Not all rock music uses four-measure phrases, but this will start you off on the right track by thinking of fills in the context of musical structure. Be sure to alternate the sticking in a right, left, right, left manner in Figure 8-4. The only exception to this is pattern number 2. Here, you must begin with the left hand. Except for number 2, each of these patterns will crash to the right of the drum kit. If you do not have a crash cymbal on your right side, use your ride cymbal. Yes, you can also crash on ride cymbals.

FIGURE 8-4: Eighth-note fills using the snare and tom-toms

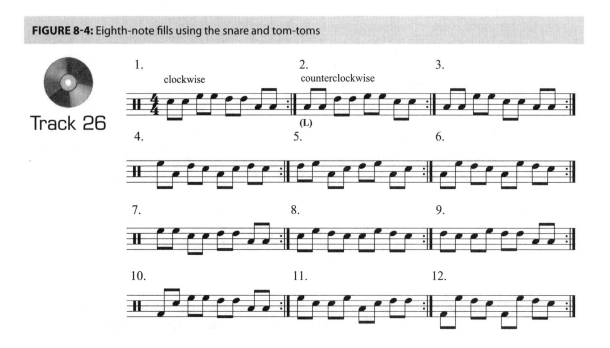

Track 26

Now, try some examples that use the snare, tom-toms, quarter notes, eighth notes, and eighth rests. These are very effective in any style of rock or pop as well as offshoots like hip-hop and modern country. Rests make fills sound less mechanical. Like most of the fills you've already played, each of these patterns should be played beginning with the right hand. You should also alternate (R, L, R, L, etc.). Come up with your own variations using

FIGURE 8-5:
Snare and tom-tom fills using quarter notes, eighth notes, and rests

quarter notes, eighth notes, and corresponding rests. You can create dozens of fills just by shifting a note or notes to a rest and vice versa. If you can sing the fill in your head, it's probably a good fill.

You're now ready to use sixteenth notes. Like Figure 8-4, pattern number 1 shows you a clockwise movement around the kit and pattern number 2 shows you a counterclockwise movement. Pattern number 2 must begin with the left hand and alternate. However, the other fills in this figure should begin with the right hand and alternate.

FIGURE 8-6: Sixteenth-note fills using the snare and tom-toms

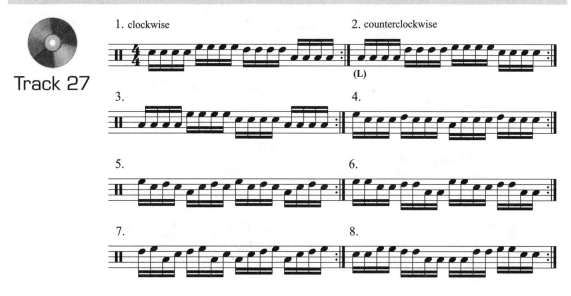

Track 27

Pattern #'s 1, 2, and 7 are played on the CD.

Like every other fill in this chapter, practice Figure 8-6 with a basic beat and four bar phrases. When doing this, be sure to play the basic beat at a slow tempo. If you start too fast, when you get to the fourth measure, the fill will be too difficult to execute. Sixteenth notes move quickly even at moderate speeds! To ensure that you're playing the beat and the fill at the same speed, always use a metronome.

The last group of fills in this section combines all that you've learned so far. In other words, these fills use quarter notes, eighth notes, dotted eighth notes, quarter rests, eighth rests, and sixteenth notes. Pattern numbers 12–14 also use sixteenth rests. All of these fills begin with the right hand and alternate. The only exception to this is number 12, which begins with the left hand.

FIGURE 8-7: Snare and tom-tom fills using a variety of duple rhythms

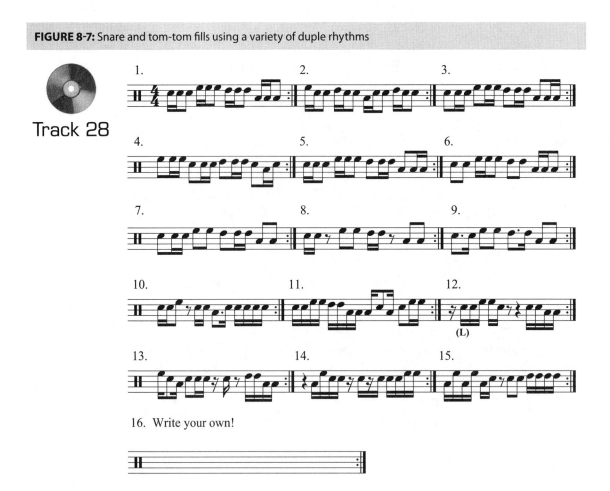

Track 28

16. Write your own!

Pattern #'s 1, 11, and 15 are played on the CD.

Figure 8-7 includes most of the rhythms (not patterns) you will need to know in order to play idiomatic rock and pop fills. The only exceptions to this are double-stroke rolls, which are thirty-second notes, and triplets. You will learn about double-stroke rolls later in this chapter, and triplets in Chapter 9.

Adding the Bass Drum

If you want to play fills like the pros, you need to know how to add the bass drum into your fills. Coordinating your right foot—assuming you're set up righty—and your hands is not easy. However, by now you should have some experience doing this, given the many beats found in Chapters 5, 6, and 7.

In Figure 8-8, look for examples where single-stroke rolls (R, L, R, L), double-stroke rolls (RR, LL), and paradiddles (RLRR, LRLL) are formed between the hands and the bass drum. Like the previous beats, the bass drum represents the "rights" in this context. However, don't take this too literally. When playing fills between the hands and feet, you mustn't ignore your right hand. Therefore, in this context, rudimental sticking rules should not be followed exactly. The goal here is to capture the feel of the rudiment through interaction between the hands and feet.

Figure 8-9 takes the ideas espoused in Figure 8-8 a step further. Here, you will see sixteenth notes primarily. Look for the use of rudiments—singles, doubles, and paradiddles—woven into these fills. Pattern number 1 is an obvious single-stroke roll between the hands and the bass drum. Pattern number 2 is a double-stroke simulation, pattern number 8 is a paradiddle,

FIGURE 8-8:
Basic fills that use the bass drum

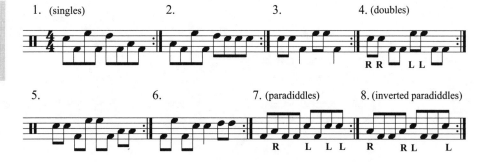

Unless otherwise indicated, all sticking begins with the right hand and alternates.

and pattern number 9 is an inverted paradiddle. You should play all single-stroke stickings on these patterns, even though doubles and paradiddles are implied in the instrumental layout. If you do this, you will get more volume, power, and consistency.

Like every fill in this chapter, you should play Figure 8-9 in the context of a basic beat. However, fills 2, 3, and 5 end with two bass drum notes and this makes getting back into the groove (basic beat) quite challenging. Therefore, play a snare hit with the crash after you complete the fill on these specific patterns. Why? Three bass drum notes in a row would be too diffi-

FIGURE 8-9: More advanced fills using the bass drum

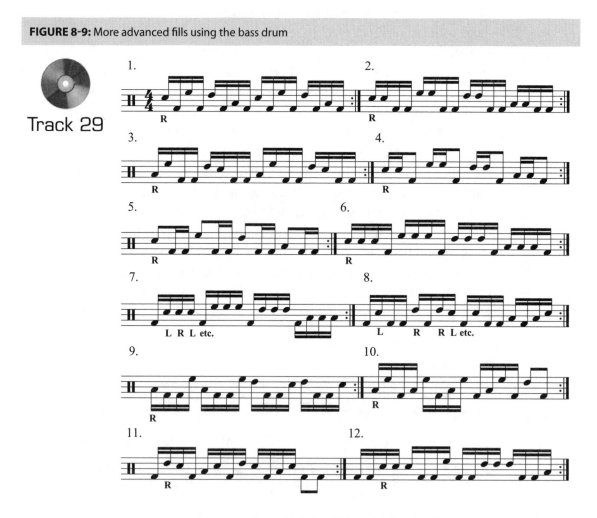

Track 29

Pattern #'s 1, 6, and 12 are played on the CD.

cult to play, unless the tempo is very slow, and naked crashes sound wimpy. Therefore, your only option is to add a snare drum on the downbeat of one in the first measure of the groove.

Incorporating Rolls

Once you learn the six basic rudiments (see Chapter 3), you should orchestrate them around the kit in both literal and implied ways. Additionally, there are other rudimental rolls, which can be turned into effective fills. These are the five-stroke, six-stroke, nine-stroke, and seventeen-stroke rolls. Other rudimental rolls exist too, but they are trickier and should be avoided for the time being.

Figure 8-10 shows you the five-stroke, six-stroke, nine-stroke, and seventeen-stroke rolls. Notice that the sticking for the six-stroke roll contains a single sticking (L, R) at the end of the roll. (The inverted six-stroke roll bookends these single strokes.) This roll also does not alternate. By contrast, the other rolls in this group begin with the right hand then switch to the left hand. It is this back and forth—right to right, left to left—sticking pattern that is termed alternating. When playing these rolls, make sure you play the correct number of strokes. To ensure this, count primary strokes (see Chapter 3). Also, make sure that each double stroke (RR or LL) is clean and articulate. You are not playing buzzes here. Finally, be sure to observe the accents.

Now, put these rolls to use in fills. As you will see, the shorthand for a five-stroke roll uses two eighth notes. The shorthand for a six-stroke roll uses one eighth and two sixteenths. This can also be inverted so the roll is written using a sixteenth-eight-sixteenth pattern. The shorthand for a nine-stroke roll uses just two quarter notes and the shorthand for a seventeen-stroke roll uses a half note and a quarter note.

Figure 8-11 gives you sixteen fills that use rolls. When playing these patterns, choose sticking that allows you to move smoothly from drum to drum. You should start each fill, however, with the right hand. If you combine rolls with various duple rhythms, you can create many more fill variations, so don't forget to experiment with your own licks too.

FIGURE 8-10: The five-stroke, six-stroke, nine-stroke, and seventeen-stroke rolls

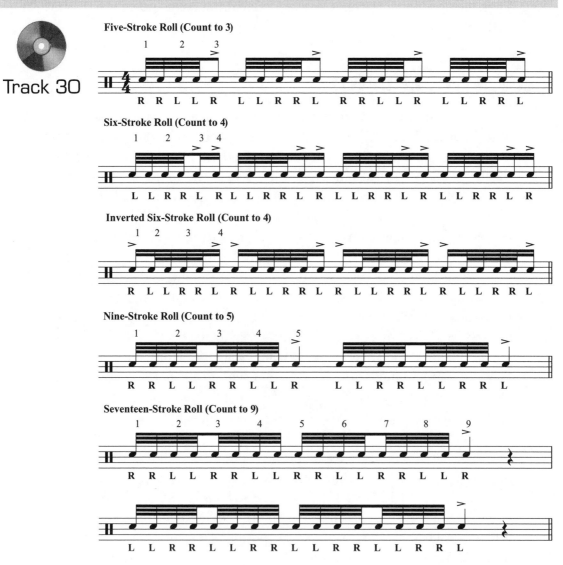

Track 30

When you count these rolls, you are counting primary strokes *not* beats in the measure!

FIGURE 8-11: Basic fills with rolls

Track 31

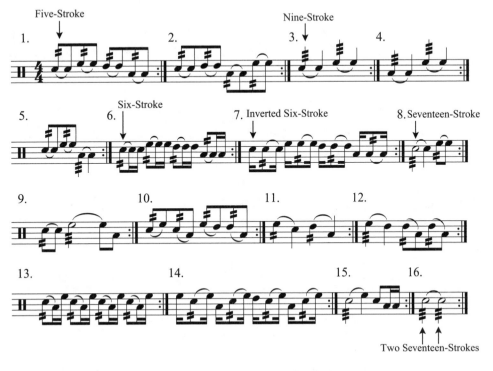

Pattern #'s 1, 7, and 14 are played on the CD.

Fills Using Flams, Ruffs, and Double Stops

Some of the best rudiments to apply to the drum set are flams and three-stroke ruffs. Figure 8-12 shows you nine fills that implement flams. Be careful to use a clean flam sound when playing these fills. In other words, make sure your grace notes do not collide with the main notes. If you're not sure what a flam is, see Chapter 3. Proper form is essential when playing this rudiment.

Flams thicken up fills quite nicely. They work best on slow songs, particularly "power ballads" or any other song form that features grandiosity. For example, on Journey's pop hit, "Open Arms," from the 1981 multiplatinum album *Escape*, drummer Steve Smith plays a wonderful flam-based fill leading the band into high gear. This is an example of power-ballad drumming at its best. This isn't to say, however, that you should only use flams on slow tempos. Drummer Stewart Copeland, of The Police, uses them all the time at fast clips. Again, just be careful not to "pop" the flam by playing the grace note and the main note at the same time. Also, notice how pattern numbers 9–12 place the grace notes on the snare and the main notes on tom-toms.

Three-stroke ruffs are also quite effective in rock and pop music. They have essentially the same effect on fills as flams do; however, the presence of two grace notes makes the main note sound even fatter. Figure 8-13 shows

FIGURE 8-12: Fills using flams

Track 32

Pattern #'s 1, 8, and 12 are played on the CD.

you some possibilities. Like Figure 8-12, select patterns (numbers 5 and 6) place the grace notes on one drum and the main notes on another.

You can combine three-stroke ruffs with flams as well. For example, you might play a three-stroke ruff on the downbeat of one then move around the kit playing sixteenth notes and end on the downbeat of four with a flam. Use your creativity and play what sounds good to you!

The last concept in this chapter deals with double stops. Double stops are extremely common in drumming, and some of the most powerful fills

FIGURE 8-13: Fills using three-stroke ruffs

Track 33

Use right-handed ruffs only on this figure!

Pattern #'s 1, 5, and 8 are played on the CD.

employ this double-surface approach. A double stop consists of two notes being played at the same time. The term is originally derived from "stopping" two notes at once on a stringed instrument such as a violin or guitar. On drums, double stops are sometimes called flat flams; however, you would never want to play double stops or flat flams on the same drum. Always place your hands on *separate surfaces*. This is not limited to drums; cymbals are considered surfaces too.

Double-stop licks are most effective when you add a crescendo (see pattern numbers 1 and 2). A crescendo is a gradual increase in volume. Eight double-stop fill options are shown to you in Figure 8-14. For a great example of double stops on the tom-toms, listen to the intro to Van Halen's "Panama" from the classic album *1984*.

FIGURE 8-14: Fills using double stops

Track 34

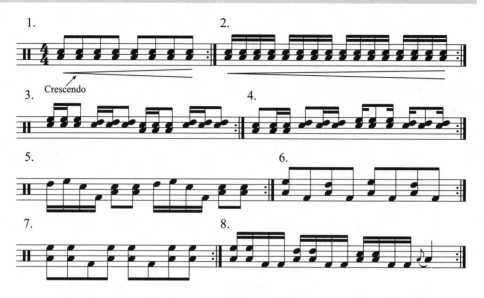

Pattern #'s 2 and 8 are played on the CD.

Chapter 9

Fancy Fills

This chapter takes fills to the next level. On the following pages, you will learn how to implement ghost notes and accents, then use triplets in a variety of ways. For example, you will orchestrate triplets around the kit then break them up between your hands and bass drum. You'll also experiment with cross sticking and learn about a subtler form of filling called beat-fill combinations. All this will give you the tools you need to fill like a pro. These fills will also prep you for improvisation and soloing.

Using Ghost Notes and Accents

You used accents in Figure 3-8, where you practiced stick control exercises. Moreover, accents accompanied the five-stroke, six-stroke, nine-stroke, and seventeen-stroke rolls in Figure 8-10. However, accents become even more exciting when you pair them up with ghost notes. In Figure 9-1, you will see fills that use both ghost notes and accents.

You first met ghost notes when working on beats. Unfortunately, ghost notes are not used enough in rock and pop music. Further, those who avoid using them tend to sound stiff and mechanical. It is true that, in rock, you will often want to play monodynamic licks. However, this is not an ironclad rule. The bottom line is that ghost notes will spice up fills in unique ways. They add dimension, texture, and nuance to your playing. Therefore, use them often.

ESSENTIAL

Listen to drummers such as Steve Gadd, Omar Hakim, Cindy Blackman, Keith Carlock, and Manu Katche, to name a few, and you will hear ghost notes being employed often. Ghost notes allow you to create meaningful phrases on the drums and help you get a sleek yet organic sound.

As mentioned earlier, ghost notes are best used in conjunction with accents. In this context, ghost notes create a noticeable dynamic contrast. When you play ghost notes and accents, the ghost notes should sound almost inaudible. In Figure 9-1, the left hand plays ghost notes while the right hand plays accents around the tom-toms and snare. (The left hand also plays accents on the snare drum in pattern numbers 2, 3, and 7.) Notice the use of three-stroke ruffs (notated with thirty-second notes) in pattern numbers 5 and 6, as well as six-stroke rolls in numbers 7 and 8. In terms of difficulty, these fills are intermediate to advanced. Therefore, take them slowly and methodically at first.

FIGURE 9-1: Fills using ghost notes and accents

Track 35

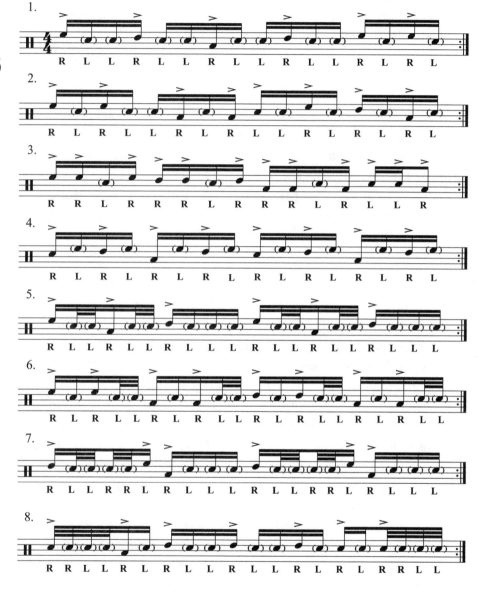

Pattern #'s 1, 5, and 8 are played on the CD.

Eighth-Note Triplets

Now it's time to shift gears and revisit an old friend: triplets. Triplet fills are common in rock, and Chapter 7 showed you how to use them in beats. They are also effective fills. However, the biggest mistake students make when playing eighth-note triplet fills is playing them out of time.

ALERT!

In drumming, if you're slightly "off" rhythmically, you are probably very off rhythmically. Drummers such as Vinnie Colaiuta, Dave Weckl, Terri Lynn Carrington, Steve Gadd, Dennis Chambers, and others have raised the bar higher than previous generations. In fact, these days, pro drummers are expected to play with (virtually) the same precision as a drum machine.

Figure 9-2 gives you an opportunity to play eighth-note triplet fills around the drum set. Begin each fill with the right hand and alternate unless otherwise directed. The first fill moves around the kit clockwise and the second fill moves in a counterclockwise direction. They are, in fact, the triplet equivalents to pattern numbers 1 and 2 in Figure 8-4 and pattern numbers 1 and 2 in Figure 8-6. In Pattern numbers 10 and 11, the sticking shifts so that the left hand plays double lefts (LL) as the right hand roams around the tom-toms. This concept should be employed often, and applied to other rhythms as well. (You had some practice with it in Figure 9-1.) The last pattern, number 12, requires you to cross your hands. Specifically, the left hand crosses over the right hand in order to play on the second-rack tom and the floor tom. This type of movement is called cross sticking.

Next, add the bass drum into the mix. In Figure 9-3, you will play eighth-note fills that use the bass drum like a fourth tom-tom. To make is more challenging, "chick" the hi-hat foot on the downbeats of two and four as you play the fill. This will help you develop four-way independence. It will also solidify your sense of time.

FIGURE 9-2:
Eighth-note triplet fills

Unless otherwise directed, begin each fill with the right hand and alternate.

Come up with your own triplet fills. To start, experiment with two triplets in the hands and one triplet in the bass drum. Move your hands around the snare and tom-toms randomly. As you do this, listen for little "melodies." Once you land on a pattern you like, refine the lick until you've developed your own signature fill.

You'll see that pattern numbers 1 and 2 in Figure 9-3 use clockwise and counterclockwise motion, respectively. If you say, one-trip-let, two-trip-let, three-trip-let, four-trip-let to count these examples, you will notice that the bass drum appears on the "let." This type of fill is very common in rock, and drummers love to play it in solos, too. It's usually played very fast. Because of this, you'll see example number 1 notated again in number 1 of Figure 9-7; only this time, the pattern is written as sextuplets.

Be careful not to lose the beat—especially your sense of one—when playing pattern number 12 in Figure 9-3. Since the triplets are divided into groups of two on this pattern, you might start hearing the rhythm as sixteenth notes. This is incorrect! Again, look for this pattern notated as sextuplets in number 4 of Figure 9-7.

FIGURE 9-3: Incorporating the bass drum

Track 36

With the exception of #2, begin each fill with the right hand and alternate.

Pattern #'s 1, 4, 8, and 12 are played on the CD.

Sextuplets Using Double Paradiddles and Single Strokes

Sixteenth-note triplets are twice the speed of eighth-note triplets, just as "regular" sixteenth notes are twice the speed of eighth notes. In most musical contexts, sixteenth-note triplets will be played fast. Since sixteenth-note triplets (or sextuplets) fly by quickly, drummers often use a RLRLRR, LRL-RLL sticking to make them sound smoother. This sticking is called a double paradiddle.

Figure 9-4 shows you the double paradiddle. The double paradiddle is not radically different from its cousin, the single paradiddle. In fact, all you need to do is add two additional single strokes (RL or LR) to the single paradiddle and the double paradiddle appears. For this reason, this rudiment could be called the para-paradiddle.

The double paradiddle is typically written as sextuplets or sixteenth-note triplets. To avoid confusion, the terms sextuplets and sixteenth-note triplets are interchangeable. Notice that the sticking for the double paradiddle begins with four single strokes then ends with a double stroke. Be sure to observe the accents (on the downbeats) as well.

FIGURE 9-4:
The double paradiddle

Once you're comfortable with the double paradiddle, apply it to the drum set. Figure 9-5 shows you four fills that use the double paradiddle as sextuplets. In this figure, the accented notes are all played with the right hand. You might try leading off with the left hand, too. This will give you some impressive-looking cross stickings. However, it will make each of these patterns much more difficult to execute cleanly. Still, this exercise is worthy of your time because one of your goals should be to learn how to navigate around your kit smoothly and without obstruction. Challenging yourself with a lot of cross-sticks helps you achieve control of your instrument. In a live setting, however, cross-sticks are not always practical or desired. So in real life, use them only when you feel they are absolutely necessary.

Now, shift gears and practice playing "power" sextuplets using only single-stroke stickings. Even though double paradiddles make sextuplets easier to play, single-stroke stickings should not be avoided altogether. Why? If you want to play extremely loud, pointed sextuplets, you must use singles. Figure 9-6 shows you sextuplet patterns that use single-stroke stickings.

As you have come to expect, the bass drum can also be added to the mix. Sextuplets between the hands and bass drum sound very impressive at fast speeds, and they can also be incorporated into solos (see Chapter 10). When playing sextuplet fills that use two bass drum notes in a row, use

FIGURE 9-5:
Sextuplet fills
using double
paradiddles

FIGURE 9-6:
Sextuplet fills
using single
strokes

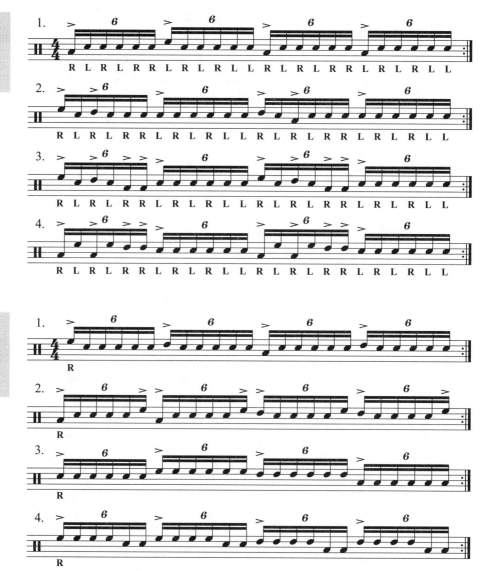

Alternate stickings on each pattern!

the heel's up-foot slide technique as described in Chapter 4. This will allow
you to play sextuplets with authority. If you're playing in a very soft context,
you can play these rhythms using the heel's-down technique too, but this is
more challenging and generally more fatiguing. See Figure 9-7 for five examples of sextuplets played between the hands and bass drum.

FIGURE 9-7: Adding the bass drum

Track 37

Alternate stickings on each pattern!
Pattern #'s 1 and 5 are played on the CD.

Blending Duple and Triple Rhythms

Blending duple and triple rhythms is tricky only insofar as they invite uneven playing and unwanted tempo swings. For the most part, triplet rhythms played back to back with eighth and sixteenth notes tend to be rushed by novice drummers. For this reason, the metronome should become your best friend when navigating your way through a sea of duple and triple combinations.

In Figure 9-8, you will see an exercise designed to help you get used to the idea of shifting back and forth between duple and triple rhythms. Apart from the obvious speed of sextuplets, and the technical challenges that go with that, they can be paired up easier with "regular" eighth and sixteenth notes. However, pairing eighth notes up with eighth-note triplets can invite trouble. Figure 9-8 helps you get used to this rhythmical union.

Next, you will play some duple and triple combinations around the drum kit. You will see that some previous concepts have also filtered their way into

Play this exercise with a metronome and repeat on loop!

these fills. For example, pattern numbers 5 and 6 use double stops. Pattern number 7 begins with a double paradiddle, and a single paradiddle is used in pattern number 8. Pattern number 9 contains a flam and an accent. The key to playing Figure 9-9 is to avoid rushing through the eighth-note triplets. Pattern number 6 is the most challenging of the batch. Here, you must delineate clearly between three eighth-note triplets and a two sixteenth-eighth duple pattern. If you're not careful, the two rhythms will begin to merge and sound the same, and this is unwanted.

FIGURE 9-9: Duple and triple combinations around the kit

Track 38

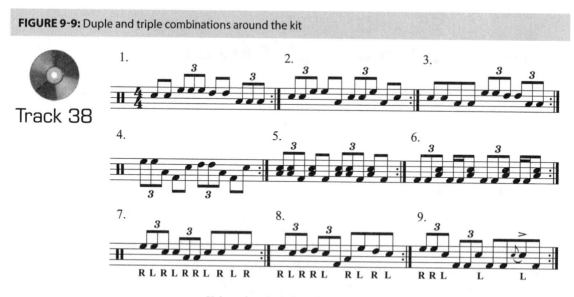

Unless otherwise indicated, start with the right hand and alternate!

Pattern #'s 1, 5, and 9 are played on the CD.

Duple and Triple Fills with Accents and Ghost Notes

This last section of triplet fills revisits accents and ghost notes. Only this time, they are paired up with both duple and triple rhythmic patterns. This includes eighth notes, sixteenth notes, eighth-note triplets, and sextuplets. The fills in Figure 9-10 are not simple. In fact, they require a fair amount of stick control to play. Further, you must be able to play with a light touch if you are to show the contrast between the ghosted notes and the accents.

E ALERT!

There are actually three dynamic levels written in Figure 9-10. They are: accents (loudest), ghost notes (softest), and the notes in between. The notes in between should be played in the middle of the dynamic spectrum. In other words, you should play them around *mf* or *mezzo forte*, which means "medium loud" in Italian.

If you're having a difficult time playing the fills in Figure 9-10, you need to go back and spend more time honing your snare drum chops. As mentioned earlier in the book, you will never play advanced (or even most intermediate) drum set material if you don't have proper stick control. Stick control means that you can play a variety of rhythms, stickings, and dynamics. Stick control is also largely concerned with precision, speed, and fluidity.

Since this chapter focuses primarily on triplets, you might ask yourself, "Where are the half-note and quarter-note triplets?" These are less common in rock, but in the right circumstance—usually dictated by tempo—rock drummers will use them. You will explore these types of triplets in Chapter 16 as you discover reggae-influenced rock. For now, focus on playing eighth- and sixteenth-note triplets accurately. Also, concentrate on playing them in combination with duple rhythms. If you master these skills, your drum fill vocabulary will be sizeable.

Other tuplets (odd groupings of notes) are also occasionally used in rock. For example, you will hear more refined players such as Bill Bruford, Terry Bozzio, and Chad Wackerman playing quintuplets (fives), septuplets (sevens), and other complex tuplet groupings in their music. Jazz, Latin, and contemporary percussionists also incorporate these rhythms. However, 99 percent of rock and pop does not require you to play such knotty rhythms, so it's best to focus on what you need to know (at least for now). In the tuplet department, that is the triplet.

FIGURE 9-10: Duple and triple-fill combinations with accents and ghost notes

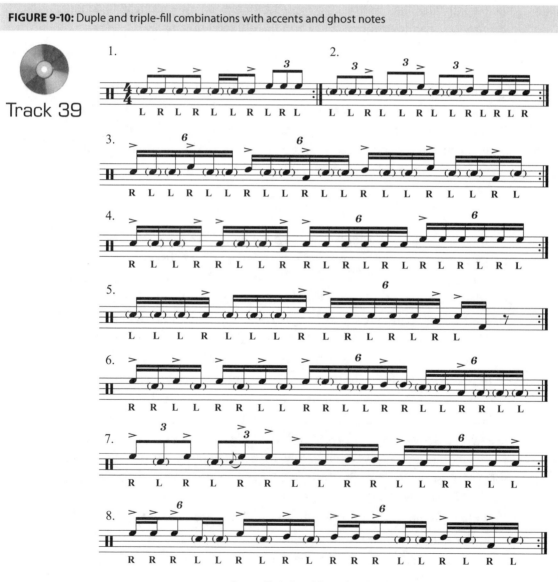

Track 39

Pattern #'s 1, 6, and 8 are played on the CD.

Beat-Fill Combinations

Beat-fill combinations are unique types of fills; they are subtler than any of the fills you have learned so far. Over the last many pages, you have learned that a fill is a separate entity from a beat. In order to play a standard fill, you must stop playing a beat. While this is often the case, it is not a must.

The tasty drummer can often find ways to anticipate the next phrase or section in a song without stopping to play a big, meaty fill. When used properly, beat-fill combinations allow the drummer to outline the structure of a song without getting too busy or intrusive. This kind of sensitivity is also a quality other musicians look for in drummers!

What is a beat-fill combination? It is just as it sounds: a mixture of a beat and a fill. To play one, vary the beat enough so it takes on some fill-like characteristics. For example, you might make the rhythm more active and you might add a tom-tom note or two. However, you must be careful not to take this too far. In other words, the groove—including the two-and-four snare backbeat—should be kept intact. If the backbeat is altered, it still must be heavily implied in some other way.

Beat-fill combinations are used when a song, or section of a song, does not require full-blown fills. When you use beat-fill combinations depends largely on preference and context. Indeed, this is where artistry and individuality come into play.

Overall, your job is to get to know the song. Think about the vocalist and the song's story. Sometimes drummers fill over key lines in the vocal, such as hooks or chorus lyrics, and this obscures the song's focus. This is a no-no. Also, big roundhouse fills sometimes break up the groove too much. If this is the case, a beat-fill combination should be used. Ultimately, it really depends on the song itself, and you must take into account what the other musicians are playing during your fill. If you don't, you're likely to step on someone's toes.

Think to yourself, "Are my fills too busy or just right?" There are many variables to consider, but the best advice is to listen closely to all the parts that are going on around you. Choose your fills based on what you're hearing and always seek to complement the music, not draw attention to the drums.

Figure 9-11 shows you ten beat-fill combinations. Harking back to the original concept of playing four-measure phrases (see Figure 8-1), this figure includes a basic beat for three bars and a beat-fill combination for one bar. To save space, the beat has only been written once. Like Figure 8-1, the crash in measure one is written in parenthesis to remind you to crash only after you repeat each beat-fill combination.

FIGURE 9-11: Beat-fill combinations

Track 40

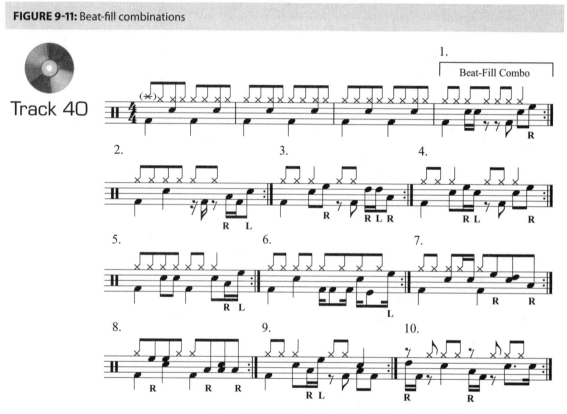

Remember to play three bars of time before each example!

Pattern #'s 1, 7, and 10 are played on the CD.

Chapter 10
Drum Solos

The fills you learned in Chapters 8 and 9 paved the way for soloing. In this chapter, you will explore phrasing, motivic or "idea" development, repetition, and structure. Moreover, you will learn how to implement "call and response" or "question and answer" into your solos. After this, you will practice using rudiments in your solos, particularly rolls, paradiddles, and flams. You will play two advanced solos at the end of this chapter; these professional-level solos encapsulate most of the concepts discussed so far in this book.

General Soloing Concepts

In a broad sense, solos are extended fills. However, if you think about solos like fills, your drumming will probably sound fragmented and choppy. Instead of brief licks with definite periods, soloing should contain longer phrases with lots of semicolons. If you listen to any great drummer, you will also hear smooth transitions between ideas, and each idea or motif will be developed to its maximum before the next idea begins. In other words, good drummers do not jump from idea to idea randomly; they slowly and methodically build each idea. In order to develop ideas, the drummer will vary rhythms or add layers and textures until the idea is fully realized.

To the listener, it may seem like the drummer is just playing anything that comes to mind in the heat of the moment. In fact, listeners often think that drummers just flail away at the kit in a haphazard, unsystematic fashion. However, the opposite is true. The seasoned drummer constructs solos based on focused, well-organized ideas cleanly executed around the kit. The process may be spontaneous, but the result is a kind of drum composition. A good solo is not just a patchwork of unrelated licks.

This is not to say that good drummers don't have any preconceived patterns ready to use. On the contrary, you cannot create a solo without any vocabulary or previously learned patterns. All professional drummers have a personalized "bag of tricks" they pull from. Given this, you should spend time developing your own signature licks. This will help you determine your own "voice" at the kit.

Repetition is also a key element in any solo. Good drummers know they do not need to play a new pattern every measure. Rather, they gradually develop one or two motifs by repeating them and slightly altering them. From an audience's perspective, jumping from lick to lick is confusing. Listeners' ears need something concrete and discernable to lock onto. Therefore, repetition becomes a crucial factor when "selling" your solo to an audience. This is especially true as the solo builds and climaxes.

Structuring a Solo

The most important element in any solo is structure. In jazz, drummers often solo over the form of the tune. For example, most bebop tunes contain a repeating thirty-two-bar form broken up into two sections, A and B. Most of the time, these sections are structured as AABA. In pop and rock, song sections are not usually referred to as A, B, and C, etc., although a few exceptions exist. For example, the band Genesis was obviously thinking of their music in terms of letter names when they wrote the song "ABACAB." On this tune, the title is derived from the song's form: ABACAB.

Of course, any song could be analyzed using letters. However, in rock and modern pop, song sections are referred to by names. More specifically, introduction, verse, prechorus, chorus, bridge, and outro replace letter delineations. Some songs also include a solo(s), interlude(s), or breakdown(s). Guitarists or keyboardists take the bulk of the solos in rock, however, drummers occasionally get the spotlight turned on them. Ringo Starr's solo on "The End" by The Beatles is a one such example (see Chapter 12). Another very famous rock drum solo is "In-a-Gadda-Da-Vida" by Iron Butterfly. On this song, drummer Ron Bushy plays a two-and-a-half-minute solo.

On *The Song Remains the Same,* a live concert film by Led Zeppelin, you will see John Bonham take an extended drum solo on "Moby Dick." Found toward the end of the film, Bonham's solo displays both ferocity and sensitivity. For portions of the solo, he even plays with his bare hands. Soloing without sticks was one of Bonham's most imitated trademarks.

Unlike bebop, virtually all solos in rock are open ended. This means they do not follow the structure of the tune. Swing-era drummers were the first to introduce the "cadenza drum solo," and much credit must be given to Gene Krupa for his exciting solo on "Sing, Sing, Sing" as performed by the Benny Goodman Orchestra. On this solo, Krupa used tom-toms to create thumping "jungle" rhythms, which proved to be quite infectious with listeners. Soon, Krupa's solo became the featured element in "Sing, Sing, Sing" eclipsing Goodman's own virtuosic clarinet playing. Such is the power of drums.

FACT

Buddy Rich, who is discussed in greater depth in Chapter 14, was the undisputed master of the cadenza drum solo, and to this day, few drummers can play with such precision, fire, and skill. Other swing-era drummers—Chick Webb, Jo Jones, Sid Catlett, Sonny Greer, and Cozy Cole—were also electrifying drum set soloists.

Does an open-ended solo imply free playing? Actually it doesn't. If you play a hodge-podge of notes and unrelated rhythmic patterns, your solo will sound unfocused, random, and undisciplined. When structuring a drum solo, you must create a beginning, middle, and end. Moreover, in most cases, the end of your solo must contain a climax. In theory, this is a simple formula. However, the reality of playing solos with a clearly defined beginning, middle, and end is not as easy as it seems.

Musical Conversations

It's best to think of a drum solo as a dialog between the various drums and cymbals of your drum kit. Call and response, also known as question and answer, is the best place to begin when creating a percussive "conversation." Think about what takes place during a conversation between two people: Generally speaking, one person makes a statement—often asking a question—and the second person replies. The question and answer are connected to one another through logic. Unless the answerer misheard the question, you would never hear a reply that has nothing to do with the question. For example, if person A asks, "Would you like a cup of coffee?" and person B responds, "Quetzal birds are beautiful in flight," the exchange would make no sense. However, if person B responded, "Yes, I would love a cup of coffee," or "No, thank you. I prefer tea," you would see the logical connection between the two statements.

A drum solo should mimic a conversation. When soloing, you should strive to create an eloquent musical statement then answer it in a logical, coherent way. When creating the "question" or "call," play a rhythm that has some melodic feel to it. Then answer your question using similar

FIGURE 10-1: Call and response

Track 41

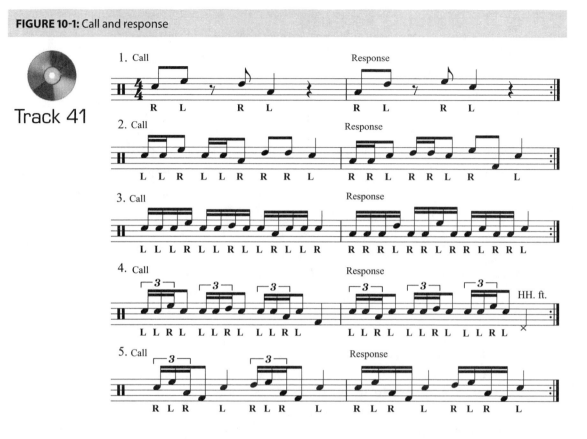

rhythms. This means playing a rhythmical variation of some sort. Often, inversions are used to create a rhythm that complements the question or call. Figure 10-1 shows you some examples of call and response in two-measure phrases. Not sure what a phrase is? A phrase is a group of notes that function as a single musical unit or event. Think of a phrase as a musical sentence.

E ALERT!

Even though rock is your focus, you should listen to drum solos by jazz drummers. Max Roach, Elvin Jones, Joe Morello, Shelly Manne, Kenny Clarke, Roy Haynes, Art Blakey, and others helped develop the highly advanced independence and four-limb coordination that professional rock players use today.

Using Rudiments to Solo

Rudiments have long been the basis for musical ideas on the drum set. For this reason, you should learn how to play each of the forty internationally recognized rudiments (see *www.pas.org*). Some rudiments are more important than others. For example, the pataflafla is not as central as each of the roll rudiments or even the more universal flam accent. However, this doesn't mean that the pataflafla won't hone your chops. At the end of the day, no rhythm or sticking is a waste of time; they are all instructive and educational. Bottom line: If it challenges you, you're learning something valuable.

As you work your way through each of the forty rudiments, don't forget about rudiment inversions/variations, too. These can be just as useful and practical as any of the rudiments included in the formal list. Check out Charles Wilcoxon's book *Modern Rudimental Swing Solos for the Advanced Drummer* for some great rudimental variations (see Appendix A).

QUESTIONS

Where can I see rudiment playing in action?
Have you ever seen a drum and bugle corp. perform? If you have, chances are, you've witnessed some of the most awesome rudimental snare drum playing on the planet. Drummers who dedicate themselves to playing "corp. style" usually have blazing fast, yet clean and precise, rudimental chops. If you haven't observed this style of drumming yet, make it a priority.

When applying rudiments to solos, begin by implementing rolls. Figure 10-2 shows you a twelve-bar drum solo that uses a variety of rolls. For ease in reading, all of the rolls have been written in long hand, meaning they are spelled out as thirty-second notes. As you reach the end of the solo, you will see some crash cymbals used in the right hand. Feel free to crash on the ride cymbal if you do not have an actual crash positioned off to your right side. You will notice the use of long rolls (aka double stroke), five-, six-, and nine-stroke rolls, plus three-stroke ruffs. You will also see two new rudiments, the seven-stroke roll (measures one and ten) and the eleven-stroke roll (measures eight and nine).

FIGURE 10-2: Using rolls

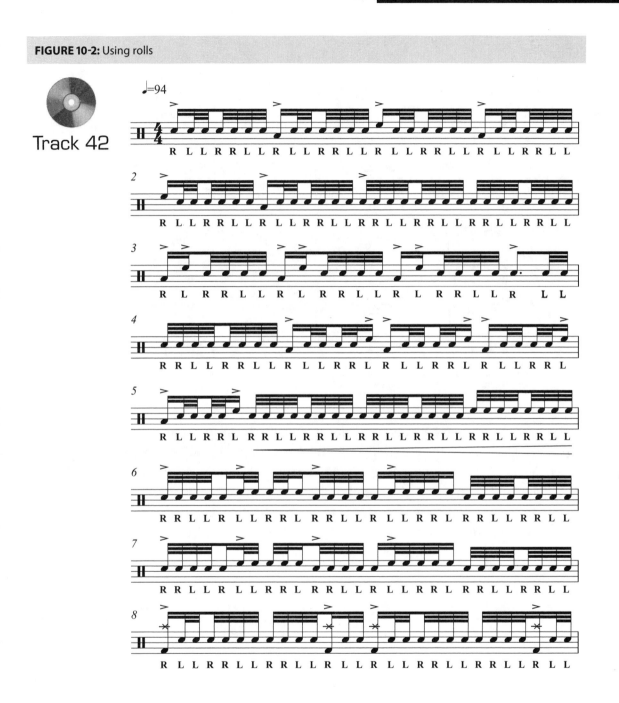

Track 42

FIGURE 10-2: Using rolls *(continued)*

Track 42

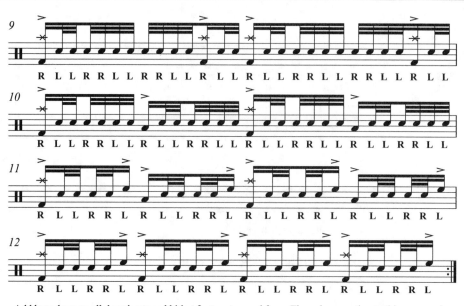

Add bass drum on all downbeats and hi-hat foot on two and four. The only exception to this occurs when the bass drum plays with the cymbal on measures 8 and 9.

As previously mentioned, any rudiment can be used as the basis for soloing. Figure 10-3 shows you a twelve-bar solo using paradiddles and flams. Take note of the flam-eighth note motif used in measures four, eight, ten, and twelve, and be careful of the triplets in measures seven and nine. As always, make sure your flams are clean. You will need to use proper form to ensure the grace note and main note don't land on top of each other, creating an unwanted flat flam.

FIGURE 10-3: Using flams and paradiddles

Track 43

Solo Etude #1: Livonia Bulldogs

Solo Etude #1: Livonia Bulldogs is a rudimental drum set solo. The best rock drummers use rudiments in all solos. Players such as Bill Bruford, Neil Peart, and Ian Paice should immediately come to mind when you think about rudimental rock drumming. Given its rudimental underpinning, you will see a lot of snare drum action in this solo, not unlike Figure 10-2, where you practiced rolls around the kit.

Many different types of rolls are employed here. Most notably, you will see the seven-stroke roll (RR, LL, RR, L–LL, RR, LL, R) used throughout. In fact, this roll shows up in measures 3, 4, 10, 11, 17–22, 24, 26, 30, and 31. The five-stroke roll is also quite pervasive, showing up in measures 1, 3, 4, 13, and 17–22. Additionally, the nine-stroke roll makes an appearance in measures 10 and 11. In fact, it appears twice in each of these measures. The first time it is used—on beats one and two—the final stroke is played in the bass drum. The same is true of measure 12, where you see a thirteen-stroke roll played between the hands and the bass drum foot.

Other rolls are also woven into this piece. First, measures 32–34 contain whole-note rolls. These rolls could be considered long rolls or generic double-stroke rolls. Secondly, the single-stroke roll appears in measures 5 and 35. Lastly, the rolls written over a dotted eighth-quarter note rhythm in measures 23, 25, and 27–29 are fifteen-stroke rolls. In all of these measures, the fifteen-stroke roll is played: R, LL, RR, LL, RR, LL, RR, LL.

Figure 10-4 gives your left hand a good workout, so be careful to play the numerous lefty sixteenth notes clean and even. Also, be sure not to rush through the sextuplets. During the long roll in measures 32–34, you don't really need to count diligently. You could interpret this roll as a hold or fermata. When you bring the roll down to a *pp* or *pianissimo dynamic,* make sure you are playing extremely soft. At its softest, your roll should sound like a whisper.

Finally, the word "Rall." shown in measure 35 stands for *rallentando.* This means to slow down gradually. When decreasing the speed, show a contrast between the first set of thirty-second notes (beat one) and the last set of thirty-second notes (beat four). The last eight notes in measure 35 should really sound more like eighth notes. Why do this? Tempo contrasts allow for more dramatic endings.

FIGURE 10-4: Solo Etude #1: Livonia Bulldogs

Track 44

Dedicated to Andrew Lawton
Livonia Bulldogs
By Eric Starr

FIGURE 10-4: Solo Etude #1: Livonia Bulldogs *(continued)*

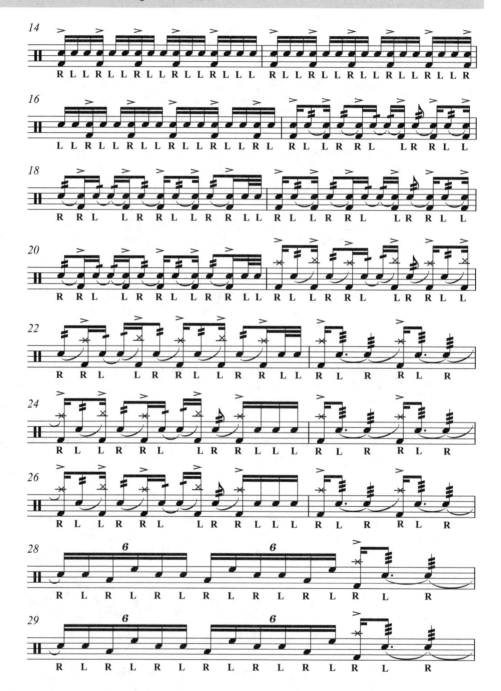

FIGURE 10-4: Solo Etude #1: Livonia Bulldogs *(continued)*

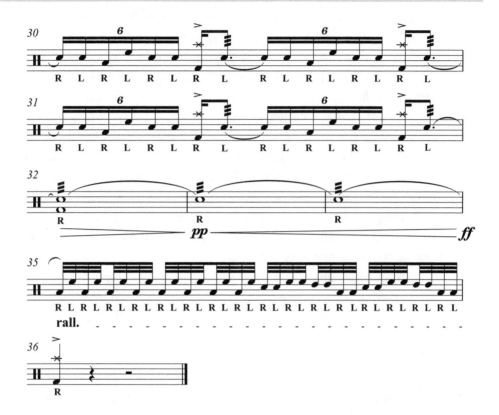

Solo Etude #2: Abel's Farewell

Figure 10-5, "Abel's Farewell," is arguably the most advanced piece in this book, as it uses a wide variety of rhythms in a nonrudimental fashion. This isn't to say that rudiments aren't played or implied. This would be virtually impossible on the drum set. However, unlike Solo Etude #1, rudimental rolls are not the focus.

This solo centers largely on two elements: double stops and sextuplets. Additionally, the hi-hat "chick" heard throughout glues the triple and duple rhythms together conceptually. You might think of the hi-hat part as a ticking clock. In contrast with Solo Etude #1, this piece lacks continuous flowing patterns. It also does not contain distinct sections or rhythmical refrains. Instead, it is built on spurts of energy followed by sudden lulls, or periods of silence. As you will find out, during the silent moments, only the hi-hat foot and a lingering crash will be heard.

Technically speaking, it's not easy playing steady quarter notes in the hi-hat foot while simultaneously playing sextuplets, sixteenth notes, and thirty-second notes overtop. However, when the music really heats up in measures 20, 23, 24, 27, 28, 31, and 33, the hi-hat is omitted, much as it would be if this solo were a spontaneous improvisation.

On the other hand, the thirty-second-note patterns in measures 23, 24, 27, 28, 31, and 33 are easier than they may look (and sound). The central motif used here is RLL, RLL, and anyone with good technique should be able to play this sticking at a pretty fast clip.

However, at 100 beats per minute, you will not be able to eyeball or scan each group of thirty-second notes in the aforementioned measures. The tempo is just too fast for this! Therefore, count and memorize the number of accents in each RLL pattern so that you play the correct number of notes in each phrase.

For example, in measures 23 and 24, you are asked to play eight RLL patterns followed by one RLLL. After this, you then move into sextuplets. Assuming you know to add an additional L after the eighth RLL pattern, you may count this accented phrase as such: 1, 2, 3, 4, 5, 6, 7, 8, 9. After the 9th count, you will play the triplets on beat four of measure 24. Remember though, count number 9 must contain an additional L. This may seem like an unorthodox approach to counting; however, this method ensures that you play the correct number of accents, and in this case, the correct number of thirty-second notes.

Use this same procedure for counting measures 27 and 28, which are rhythmically identical to measures 23 and 24. However, for this phrase you should count 1, 2, 3, 4 on the high tom then move to the snare drum and count 1, 2, 3, 4, 5. Again, this assumes that you understand count #5 contains an extra L. The reason the count is broken up into 4 + 5 is you need to maneuver between the high tom and the snare drum. If you don't break up the count, you may become confused and linger on the high tom too long or move to the snare drum prematurely. This counting method also works with measures 31 and 33, where the accents move clockwise and counterclockwise around the kit.

The accent counting method described in this chapter works in any situation where you are asked to play a static rhythm for a set period of time. Remember though, it works only when you are asked to play fast repeating patterns with accentuation. When you use this method, you're assuming that the accent is the first note of each pattern.

Like any solo, practice Figure 10-5 (Solo Etude #2) at a slow tempo until the sticking and orchestrations around the kit become smooth and natural. Ultimately, it's a good idea to memorize all of the solos found in this chapter, or partially memorize them, so the music serves only as a kind of cheat sheet.

As you probably know, rock drummers never read a solo. Ultimately, use the solos found in this chapter as food for thought and inspiration for your own improvisational ideas. The objective with each figure is to build limb independence and stick control so that, in turn, you learn how to create your own unique and exciting solos.

With this in mind, a simple motif is provided for you in Figure 10-6. Try building a solo around this motif, which is purposely plain and wide open to interpretation. Remember, your ideas needn't be complex, just cohesive and logical. On the CD, you will hear one way to improvise over this motif. On the recording, the focus is sextuplet rhythms but you may choose a wide variety of approaches. Be creative and have fun exploring your own ideas.

FIGURE 10-5: Solo Etude #2: Abel's Farewell

FIGURE 10-5: Solo Etude #2: Abel's Farewell *(continued)*

Track 45

FIGURE 10-5: Solo Etude #2: Abel's Farewell *(continued)*

Track 45

FIGURE 10-6: Improvising over a simple motif

Track 46

Chapter 11

Funky Drumming

In this chapter, you will explore the funkier side to drumming. It begins with a brief history and definition of funk, including a key term called the "deep pocket." Next, you will receive helpful hints on how to avoid overplaying, and you will learn about James Brown's inimitable song, "Funky Drummer." From there, you will study alternate ride ostinatos and even learn how to use two ride surfaces at once. All this will add depth and color to your drumming, and your overall musical vocabulary will grow.

History of Funk Music

Around 1965, funk emerged in the United States as a distinct genre. It culled from the African American experience and it borrowed from rhythm and blues, rock 'n' roll, soul, jazz, and by the late '60s, psychedelic rock. On drums, New Orleans second-line contributed indirectly to funk's rhythmical development. This traditional style of parade drumming contains syncopations, backbeats, repetition, and a subtle swing or shuffle feel. Today, these musical elements are at the heart of funk drumming. For example, check out the drumming styles of Zigaboo Modeliste, Johnny Vidacovich, and Stanton Moore.

Funk was and is primarily "jam" oriented. Funk rhythm sections often hang on one chord—even one rhythmical ostinato—while horns add punchy, repetitive lines overtop. It's also not uncommon for a singer(s) to riff on a catchy lyrical theme. James Brown's "Get Up Offa That Thing" is one example of this. Another instance is Parliament's "Give Up the Funk (Tear the Roof Off the Sucker)." The Average White Band's "Pick Up the Pieces" is yet another funk example that features horns and a vocal riff. In this case, the horns play a recurring melody while the song title is chanted occasionally in the background.

FACT

Funk is not known for its brevity. On the contrary, most funk artists use lengthy jams, which give the music the feel of a loop. It's not surprising that classic funk, from the '60s and '70s, has been appropriated by contemporary hip-hop artists. In this sense, hip-hop and funk share a common bond.

In funk, one-chord vamps become hypnotic, and for most tunes, the groove remains unchanged. Sometimes dynamics are used, but the drums and bass may sustain long stretches of timekeeping at a single volume. Abrupt tempo shifts are rare, and rubato playing is never used in the body of a funk song. These musical elements would destroy the very fabric—the groove—of the music. In short, funk is based on steady, repetitive timekeeping from beginning to end. This makes the music infectious, energizing, and most of all, danceable.

Today, the term funk is rather generic. Often, it is used to describe *any* groove with a steady R&B-influenced backbeat. More and more, funky elements are popping up in many styles of rock and pop. For example, it's not uncommon to hear funk used in alternative rock and even certain forms of heavy metal. And musicians employ the term "funky" quite casually. Often, it will be used in conjunction with another phrase: the "deep pocket."

Defining the Deep Pocket

You could say that the deep pocket is musicians' slang for playing a drum and bass groove that *feels really good*. However, the question arises: How do you define feel? Usually, feel is defined by steadiness and intent. Wavering, tentative playing never feels good. Clean, articulate playing further enhances good feel; sloppy musicianship never feels good either. However, articulate performances should not be confused with mechanical or stiff playing. Despite the obvious mechanics used to play a groove, a drumbeat should always sound relaxed and effortless. In other words, the music should sound like it's playing itself. When this occurs, the deep pocket has been established.

This term is best understood by listening to music that epitomizes it. Below, you will see a brief list of tunes that have great feel. These songs are definitely in the deep pocket. Can you think of others? There are many, many more. When you listen to music, think about feel and ask yourself, "Are the bass and drums in the pocket, or are they wavering and hesitant?"

The songs below are listed chronologically and run the gamut from early rock 'n' roll to soul to pop to modern rock.

1. "The Fat Man" (1949, Fats Domino; found on numerous "greatest hits" collections; the drummer is Earl Palmer.)
2. "Hound Dog" (1956, Elvis Presley; found on numerous "greatest hits" collections; drummer is D.J. Fontana.)
3. "Papa's Got a Brand New Bag" (1965, James Brown; found on numerous "greatest hits" collections; drummer is Melvin Parker.)

4. "Hey Joe" (1966, Jimi Hendrix; album is *Are You Experienced*; drummer is Mitch Mitchell.)

5. "Since I've Been Loving You" (1970, Led Zeppelin; album is *Led Zeppelin III;* drummer is John Bonham.)

6. "Superstition" (1972, Stevie Wonder; album is *Talking Book;* drummer is Stevie Wonder.)

7. "If You Love Somebody Set Them Free" (1985, Sting; album is *Dream of the Blue Turtles;* drummer is Omar Hakim.)

8. "Nick of Time" (1989, Bonnie Raitt; album is *Nick of Time;* drummer is Ricky Fataar.)

9. "Sunny Came Home" (1996, Shawn Colvin; album is *A Few Small Repairs;* drummer is Shawn Pelton.)

10. "Too Much" (1996, Dave Matthews Band; album is *Crash;* drummer is Carter Beauford.)

11. "Give it Away" (2000, Red Hot Chili Peppers; album is *Blood Sugar Sex Magik;* drummer is Chad Smith.)

12. "Peaceful World" (2001, John Mellencamp; album is *Cuttin' Heads;* drummer is Steve Jordan.)

How to Avoid Overplaying

Some drummers think *play funky* means *play complex*. This is a misconception, and in fact, complex or busy playing can destroy the feel of any funky tune. Funk doesn't come from a lot of notes. Again, it comes from *feel*. The first beat in this book—a basic kick-snare, kick-snare combination—could be a funk beat in the right hands. Indeed, it has been used on scores of funky tunes. What makes it funky is the inflection the drummer puts into the beat, together with steadiness and intent. Drummers often talk about getting a "black" feel. Feel is actually colorblind; anyone can do it. But how?

Playing lots of notes and excessive syncopations is not the key to funky drumming. That is simply overplaying. The funky drummer knows how to pare down the groove to its simplest components without causing the groove to sound bare or empty.

The song "Funky Drummer" by James Brown (released on the compilation *In the Jungle Groove*) is one example of funk drumming at its finest.

This song is very instructional not because of what is played, but because of what is not played.

"Funky Drummer" was recorded in 1970 and features Clyde Stubblefield, one of funk's most celebrated drummers. There is a famous drum breakdown found halfway through the tune. James Brown introduces the break with the advice, "You don't have to do no soloing brother, just keep what you got." This is great advice. The moral? When you're playing something that's really in the pocket, there's no need to change it or get fancy. The old adage, "If it ain't broke, don't fix it" definitely applies here.

During the breakdown and throughout the song, Stubblefield uses sixteenth notes in the hi-hat. He also employs subtle note variation. Specifically, he uses hi-hat openings and buzz strokes in the snare, which add depth and color. However, Stubblefield never alters the underlying groove, or feel, of the music. This is the key element. Focus on groove and feel, not fancy licks or lots of notes; it's the placement of the notes that counts, not the quantity of notes used. The basic idea behind or *essence* of Stubblefield's breakdown is shown in Figure 11-1.

FIGURE 11-1: "Funky Drummer" idea

The open hi-hats are optional ad lib.
Also, experiment with occasional buzz strokes!

Note: This is NOT an actual transcription.

If you listen to the recording of "Funky Drummer," you will notice that Clyde Stubblefield's drums are tuned tightly. This crisp, taut sound was very common in funk in the late 1960s and early 1970s. When tuned high, the thin drum shells from this period resonate quite beautifully.

Stubblefield's breakdown is one of the most sampled rhythmical patterns in history. For example, Sinead O'Connor used a loop of his beat on her song, "I Am Stretched On Your Grave" from her seminal album *I Do Not Want What I Haven't Got.* Sampling is the process of capturing a musical snippet—often a drum and bass groove—through a digital software program on a computer. Once a segment has been extracted, it is set on loop in a new musical context. Sampling can also be achieved through tape splicing, but this technique is largely out of date today.

Alternate Ride Ostinatos

In Figure 11-1, you experimented with a sixteenth-note hi-hat ride ostinato. This ostinato can be played with the right hand at slower speeds, but it cannot be played at medium-to-fast tempos unless you change the sticking. Therefore, if you wish to play a sixteenth-note hi-hat ostinato at medium-to-fast speeds, you must alternate your sticking in a right, left, right, left fashion.

Figure 11-2 shows you some beats that use an alternating R, L, R, L sticking. When you play the snare drum—be it on a downbeat or a syncopation—you must omit the hi-hat, just like you did on beats 6–8 in Figure 7-4. Given the sticking in Figure 11-2, the snare will be played with the right hand if it occurs on a downbeat or an upbeat. If it occurs on an "e" or "ah" it will be played with the left hand, which crosses under the right hand when hitting the snare. Again, this sticking is used for medium-to-fast speeds. In Figure 11-2, the bass drum is not varied until numbers 9–12. This will allow you to focus on your hands and the ride ostinato.

FACT

While not a funk drummer, Larry Mullen Jr. from U2 often plays deep-pocketed beats with alternating sixteenth-note hi-hat ostinatos. "Sunday Bloody Sunday," "Gloria," "Pride (In the Name of Love)," and others show the precision of Mullen's sixteenth-note riding. Often, these patterns complement the percussive, motoric guitar playing of band mate The Edge.

FIGURE 11-2: Alternating sixteenths on the hi-hat

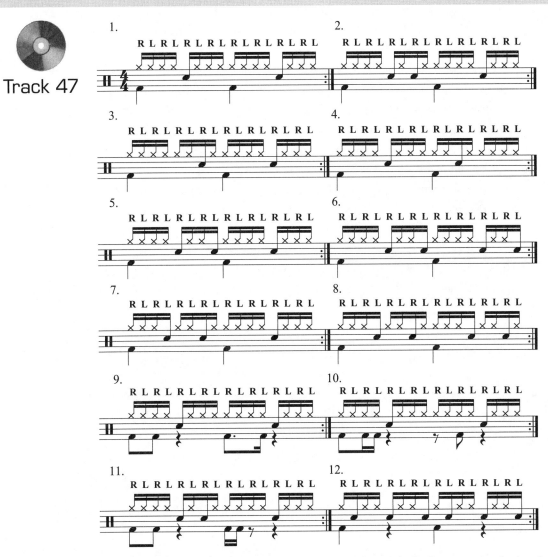

Track 47

When played at a medium tempo these beats sound funky. At fast speeds, they become more rock-oriented.

Pattern #'s 1, 7, and 12 are played on the CD.

You may also combine eighth and sixteenth notes to create additional ride ostinatos. The following patterns can be played on the hi-hat or the ride cymbal as you wish. Depending on the song, they might even have some application broken up around the tom-toms or just on the floor tom. If you don't know this yet, your tom-toms are not just for fills; they can also be used as a ride surface. Tunes such as "Sunshine of Your Love" by Cream (with drummer Ginger Baker) and "Spoonman" by Soundgarden (with drummer Matt Cameron) are two examples of tom-tom riding.

Figure 11-3 utilizes the now-familiar two sixteenths-eighth pattern, but here it is implemented as a ride. This pattern should be embedded in your musical vocabulary by now. However, transferring it to your ride surface will require some patience and attention to detail. Go slowly and remember to read each pattern vertically (see Introduction).

Figure 11-4 inverts the previous ostinato so that the eighth note is played first. This inversion is harder to play and poor stick control will mean rushed, or otherwise sloppy, rhythms. Make sure there are no flams heard

FIGURE 11-3: Two sixteenths-eighth ride pattern

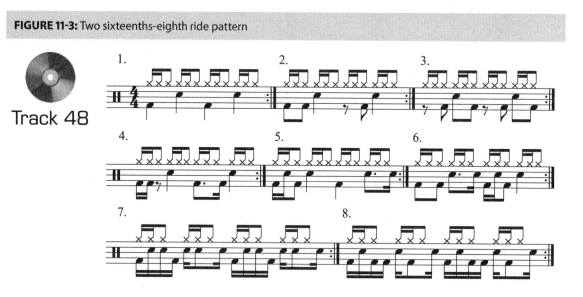

Track 48

For an extra challenge, add open hi-hats on the eighth notes!

Pattern #'s 1, 5, and 8 are played on the CD.

between the ride hand and the snare or the ride hand and the bass drum. In order to make these rhythms sound funky, you will need to play them with perfect alignment. Remember, sloppy playing does not place you in the deep pocket. In this figure, notice how numbers 7 and 8 set the two sixteenth-eighth rhythmical combination against the eighth-two sixteenth ride pattern.

FIGURE 11-4: Eighth-two sixteenths ride pattern

Track 49

For an extra challenge, add open hi-hats on the eighth notes!
Pattern #'s 1, 6, and 8 are played on the CD.

There are some other fun ride patterns you may experiment with. In Figure 11-5, four ostinatos are given to you. The first two (quarter notes and off-beats) are extremely common, and you should go back through the beats in Chapters 5–7 and play each pattern using these ostinatos. Ostinato number 3 from Figure 11-5 is really a variation on the ride pattern in Figure 11-4, and ostinato number 4 has a Latin flair to it. The latter is best used in conjunction with ghost notes and accents. Figure 11-6 shows you one possible usage.

FIGURE 11-5:
Other funky
ride ostinatos

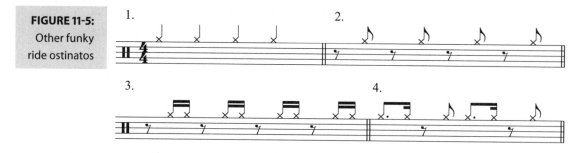

Play on HH or ride cymbal!

FIGURE 11-6:
Funk beat
with accents
and ghost
notes

Using the Cymbal Bell

Riding on the cymbal bell is very common in funk, rock, and pop. Up until now, however, you have only used the body (or bow) of the cymbal and the edge for crashing. The bell has many uses in music, too. Basically, the sky's the limit. Be creative in implementing this sound and listen for it in recordings. All the great drummers use their cymbal bells from time to time.

When playing on the ride cymbal, you will generally use a thumb's-up finger position, as opposed to the palm-flat position, which is used when playing on the snare drum. If you're unfamiliar with these terms, see Chapter 3. There are two ways to hit the cymbal bell. The first is with the tip or bead of the stick. This gets a lighter, subtler tone. For an example of this, listen to The Beatles "Don't Let Me Down" from *Let it Be*. Here, Ringo Starr plays a combination of eighth and sixteenth notes on the bell. For a heavier or chunkier sound, you must turn your wrist in the palm-flat position then strike the bell with the shaft of the stick. An example of this sound is found on Sting's "Children's Crusade" from *Dream of the Blue Turtles,* where Omar Hakim plays offbeats or "ands" in 3/4 time.

Often, when the shaft of the stick is used to strike the cymbal bell, it is applied in conjunction with four specific ostinatos. All four of these patterns are funky when executed cleanly. The first ostinato, Figure 11-7, shows you beats that use quarter notes on the bell. You can also use the tip of the stick for these beats.

As previously mentioned, offbeats are also used on the bell. The offbeat ostinato was first given to you in number 2 of Figure 11-5. Offbeats are particularly effective on the bell of the cymbal and these types of grooves have become popular in jazz-funk. See Figure 11-8 for beats that utilize an offbeat bell ostinato.

You may also take the ride patterns from Figures 11-3 and 11-4 and use the bell on the eighth-note component of the rhythm. Four beats are shown in Figure 11-9 using both ride types of ostinatos. Accuracy is important here. If the bell/body ride pattern gets bungled, the groove will suffer. Also, you'll find that the natural tendency is to accent the eighth notes on the bell. This is okay and even desirable. Therefore, accents have been written in.

If you're having trouble putting together the two sixteenth-eighth pattern and or the eighth-two sixteenth ostinato, try a simpler alternating ostinato using all eighth notes. This pattern is shown in Figure 11-10. Like before, the bell notes are written with accents.

FIGURE 11-7: Quarter-note patterns using the cymbal bell

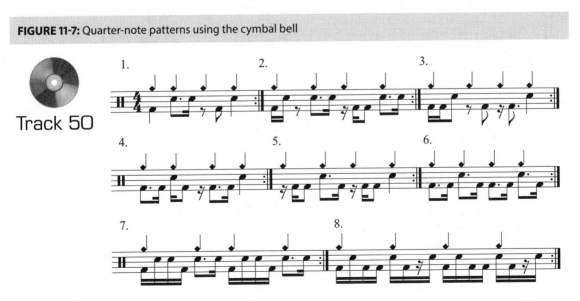

Track 50

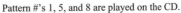

Pattern #'s 1, 5, and 8 are played on the CD.

FIGURE 11-8: Offbeat patterns using the cymbal bell

Track 51

Pattern #'s 1, 5, and 8 are played on the CD.

FIGURE 11-9: Using the body and bell of the cymbal

Track 52

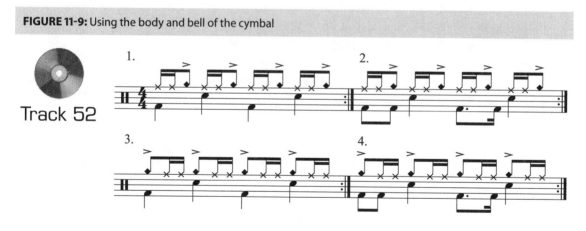

Pattern #'s 1 and 3 are played on the CD.

FIGURE 11-10:
Alternating
bell/body ride
ostinato

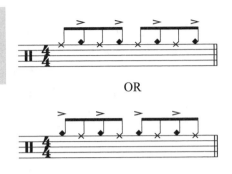

OR

Two-Handed Riding

The term, "two-handed riding" usually implies riding on two separate surfaces. Usually, these surfaces are the hi-hat and the ride cymbal. As you might guess, this is the most complex form of riding. Using both hands to ride and play backbeats is challenging, but it's not impossible. Begin by playing single strokes between the hands on the ride cymbal and the hi-hat. Then add alternating quarter notes between the bass and snare drums. When you play the snare drum there will be no cymbal or hi-hat accompaniment. In other words, the snare will be bare.

When riding with hands on separate surfaces, place your right hand on the cymbal and your left hand on the hi-hat. This is illustrated in Figure 11-11. The first example (A) uses eighth notes and the second example (B) employs sixteenth notes. The latter is more common. Notice how the right hand moves to the snare drum to play the downbeats of two and four.

FIGURE 11-11:
Basic two-
handed ride
patterns

Now, try some two-handed ride combinations that initially vary the sticking and then the rhythms themselves. This is demonstrated in Figure 11-12. Many rudiments are used in this figure. For instance, a double-stroke sticking is used in #1. Single paradiddles are used in #2, and a paradiddle inversion is employed in #3. Additionally, #5 combines single strokes with a paradiddle inversion. Be careful with numbers 6–8, as they incorporate thirty-second notes.

FIGURE 11-12: Various two-handed ride patterns

Track 53

Pattern #'s 1 and 7 are played on the CD.

One of the best examples of two-handed riding is Manu Katche's funky performance on "Somewhere Down the Crazy River" on Robbie Robertson's self-titled album (1987). Listen for other examples of two-handed riding in music. (There are many.) This approach spices up songs with tasty colors and textures. But in order to play these patterns well, you must maintain a light feel. In other words, you must perform with great finesse.

Chapter 12
1960s Innovators

In this chapter, you will learn about drummers who began their professional careers in the 1960s. The years 1960–1969 were a pivotal time for rock. During this decade, rock drumming took on a whole new personality. Much of this was due to drummers Hal Blaine, Ringo Starr, Charlie Watts, John Densmore, Mitch Mitchell, Keith Moon, Ginger Baker, Carmine Appice, Mick Avory, and a handful of other notables. All of these drummers came of age during the 1960s: a time of rebellion, shifting societal morays, and deep musical change.

Hal Blaine

Hal Blaine (born 1929) is a pop and rock giant. He is among the most recorded drummers in history, and his playing can be heard on dozens of #1 hits. From The Beach Boys' "I Get Around" to Sonny & Cher's "I Got You Babe" to Frank Sinatra's "Strangers in the Night," Blaine was at the forefront of rock and pop throughout the 1960s and first half of the 1970s. In fact, few drummers can claim to have worked with so many music legends. Among them, Blaine recorded with Elvis Presley, Dean Martin, The Supremes, Bobby Darin, Simon & Garfunkel, Neil Diamond, The Mamas & the Papas, and John Denver.

Born in Holyoke, Massachusetts, Blaine grew to prominence in the early 1960s as a first-call Los Angeles session drummer. Eventually, Blaine and other session greats of the era were nicknamed "The Wrecking Crew." This sobriquet was given to the players who dominated the LA studio scene in the 1960s. In addition to Blaine, unofficial members of The Wrecking Crew included Tommy Tedesco (guitar), Carol Kaye (bass), Glen Campbell (guitar), and about twenty others. By Blaine's calculations, The Wrecking Crew played on some 35,000 songs!

As a member of The Wrecking Crew, Blaine was largely associated with the producer Phil Spector. Additionally, he appears on The Beach Boys' seminal works. Blaine was not a flashy drummer. In fact, he never stole the spotlight; instead, his focus was always on playing tight grooves. To this end, Blaine was

FIGURE 12-1:
"Everybody
Loves
Somebody
Sometimes"
patterns

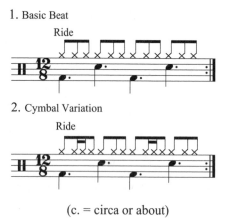

(c. = circa or about)

a masterful accompanist and his playing ultimately helped propel the melody or lead vocal. His sensitive, tasty approach to pop music is underscored by elegant stick control and creative use of colors around the drum kit.

Blaine's drumming on the Dean Martin classic "Everybody Loves Somebody Sometimes" is one example of his tasteful timekeeping. This song is a 12/8 ballad. That means that there are twelve beats in a measure and the eighth note equals one beat. (12/8 could also be written in 4/4 using eighth-note triplets.) Figure 12-1 shows you Blaine's basic beat for "Everybody Loves Somebody Sometimes." Moreover, one cymbal variation is included here. The beats in Figure 12-1 are quite common. In fact, you will hear them used on hundreds of 12/8 ballads.

On Roy Orbison's "Oh, Pretty Woman" Blaine uses a rock beat that includes a snare drum pulse on all four downbeats. He also plays some smooth, relaxed fills throughout this tune. Purchase this single and listen to how effortless and flowing this drumtrack is. This pattern is also very common in Motown; you will hear it on dozens of tracks.

FIGURE 12-2: "Oh, Pretty Woman" patterns

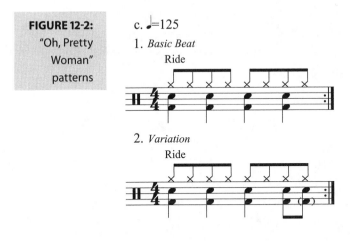

Ringo Starr

The Beatles' drummer, Ringo Starr (born 1940), may be the most underrated and misunderstood drummer in rock. Other instrumentalists and singers praise his playing, but drummers often knock his work, complaining that he has no chops. It is true that Starr could never compete in a drum battle with Buddy Rich or many of today's phenoms; however, this doesn't mean that his drumming with The Beatles isn't superb. In fact, fancier or "hotter" drummers might have overplayed on those classic albums, ruining the character of the music.

Starr was a creative parts drummer who devised beats that have now become part of the standard "groove bank" that all drummers cull from. He has also both directly and indirectly affected the way contemporary drummers *feel* rock and pop. Who could deny such deep grooves as "Hold Me Tight," "Help," "Sgt. Pepper's Lonely Hearts Club Band," "You Never Give Me Your Money," and "Don't Let Me Down" to name a few? Most good drummers performing today have a little bit of Starr in them, whether they like it or not.

One major contribution Starr made to rock drumming was the use of half-open hi-hat. It would be hard to prove that he was the first to use this technique, but he is one the earliest proponents of this "washy" sound, which is now used regularly by rock drummers of every style.

Modern rock drummers have also largely appropriated Starr's simple but perfectly crafted tom-tom fills. Yet few can truly capture the swing and nuance of Starr's approach. Starr may not have had technical prowess, but he always made the music feel great.

The song "In My Life," from *Rubber Soul,* is a brilliant example of Starr's creative parts writing. On this tune, Starr plays an inventive beat that uses an accented hi-hat note. It would have been easier (but more blasé) to play a standard kick-snare groove on this song with an eighth-note hi-hat pulse. Instead, Starr uses a more imaginative approach. Figure 12-3 shows you the basic idea behind the beat used for this song.

Another great groove by Starr is heard on "Oh! Darling" from the album *Abbey Road.* Here, Starr uses eighth notes and open hi-hats to create a beat that is texturally thick and expressive. The groove idea he uses on the verses is shown in Figure 12-4. This song is also played in 12/8 time. (See text that corresponds to Figure 12-1.)

FIGURE 12-3:
"In My Life"
verse idea

Note: This is NOT an actual transcription.

FIGURE 12-4:
"Oh! Darling"
verse idea

Play the 16th notes relaxed and with a loose grip!

Note: This is NOT an actual transcription.

John Lennon's song "Come Together" (*Abbey Road*) features an interesting beat on the introduction and reintroduction sections. On this tune, Starr plays the hi-hat and tom-toms in a distinctive way. Figure 12-5 captures the basic idea of Starr's beat. The exact use of tom-toms is not represented here.

Finally, no mention of Ringo Starr would be complete without a nod to his one and only drum solo. It appears on the song "The End" (*Abbey Road*). A spinoff of this solo is notated in Figure 12-6. Notice how the bass drum is kept steady (using eighth notes) while the hands solo overtop on the tom-toms. It's difficult to tell if Starr is using both hands (double stops) for the last two beats of the solo. However, double stops have been written here since it adds to the climax.

FIGURE 12-5:
"Come Together"
intro idea

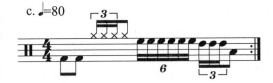

FIGURE 12-6:
"The End"
drum-solo
spinoff

c. ♩=117

Note: This is NOT an actual transcription.

Charlie Watts

The Rolling Stones' Charlie Watts (born 1941) is another drummer who is underrated by players obsessed with speed and technical virtuosity. But again, who could deny such deep-pocketed grooves as "Under My Thumb," "Jumping Jack Flash," "Brown Sugar," "Beast of Burden," or "Start Me Up"?

Charlie Watts is a smooth groove player, and his straightforward style has propelled the Rolling Stones since 1963 (1960s albums *Aftermath, Beggars Banquet,* and *Let it Bleed* solidified their eminence in rock). Sometimes, Watts omits the hi-hat on the downbeats of two and four when he keeps time. This has been criticized as bad technique by some. However, there are clear benefits to this approach. For example, a basic rock beat takes on a slightly different characteristic when the snare drum is heard by itself on beats two and four. In this case, the missing hi-hat note highlights the snappiness of the snare. Also, lifting your ride hand while playing snare backbeats helps you play louder on the drum. This is especially useful if you play traditional grip like Watts. Figure 12-7 shows you this groove idea with hi-hat omissions.

FIGURE 12-7:
Rock beat
with hi-hat
omissions

Most of the songs referenced in this chapter were recorded in the 1960s. However, a few exceptions have been made where key performances from another decade best define the drummer being analyzed. In these cases, release dates appear in parenthesis after the album title to avoid any confusion.

Arguably, Watts's finest groove is heard on "Beast of Burden" from *Some Girls* (1978). Watts never plays fancy beats, so on paper his grooves don't look like much. But given the right feel, they come alive. On the introduction to this song, you will hear a two-bar phrase that uses offbeats in the snare drum. Watts also uses these offbeats at the end of phrases in the body of the tune. He also throws in some funky hi-hat openings on the "ands" of beats one and three ad lib. Watts's basic idea, with the offbeats in the snare and the hi-hat, is illustrated in Figure 12-8. However, he varies this groove ad lib throughout the song.

Watts is also known for playing slightly behind the beat. This he does on virtually every Rolling Stones tune. The result is a relaxed, funky feel. Drummers who play on top of the beat give the music a kind of nervous tension. This is desirable when playing punk or ska. However, for music that is blues

FIGURE 12-8:
"Beast of
Burden" idea
with offbeats

Note: This is NOT an actual transcription.

or country based—like most Rolling Stones tunes—a laid-back approach is required. Check out Watts's carefree country shuffle on the song "Far Away Eyes" from the album *Some Girls*. This beat uses a lazy triplet ride pattern and a cross stick. This groove is not unique to Watts. If you do your research, you will hear this groove on dozens of other country ballads. See Figure 12-9 for the idea behind Watts's slow country shuffle.

FIGURE 12-9:
"Far Away Eyes" slow country shuffle idea

c. ♩=94

Use a cross stick on the rim of the snare!

FACT

To play a cross stick, turn your drumstick around and place it perpendicular to the snare drum rim. As you do this, the butt of the stick should be suspended perpendicularly off the right side of the drum. Using your wrist, "click" the stick shaft on the rim. You will want to find the "sweet spot" on the shaft. This exists about 3.5" from the butt end of the stick.

Watts uses some funky snare drum fills on "Start Me Up" from *Tattoo You* (1981) that also demonstrate his loose, easygoing feel. On this tune, he fills on the snare drum using accented and nonaccented eighth notes. The two basic motivic ideas for these fills are illustrated in Figure 12-10. When you play this, be sure to grip the sticks loosely.

FIGURE 12-10:
"Start Me Up" fill motifs

c. ♩=120

John Densmore

John Densmore (born 1944) was an influential West Coast rock drummer who played with The Doors. Fronted by the mercurial Jim Morrison, The Doors became one of the most popular American bands in the 1960s and beyond. Densmore's style and sound borrowed largely from jazz. For example, he was influenced by legends Elvin Jones and Dave Tough. He even portrayed the latter in a stage play called *Bad Dreams and Bebop*.

Densmore's jazzy drumming is best heard on "The End" from the album *The Doors*. On this tune, he rides on the cymbal and plays syncopated rhythmical jabs, evoking the spirit of Elvin Jones. Throughout the song, Densmore also creates rich colors on the ride cymbal by hitting different areas of the bell, bow, and edge. He also uses great dynamic contrast. He generally plays quiet on this tune. However, he throws in sudden tom-tom "bombs" and other unexpected rhythmical flurries to keep it interesting. All this adds up to a beautiful, almost entrancing, musical flow. Figure 12-11 shows you the basic idea, which uses a cross stick. Densmore plays around with this groove ad lib. Here, the simple underlying pattern is shown. If you listen to the song, you will hear lots of variations and improvisations.

Another famous beat is the opening to "Break On Through (To The Other Side)," also from the album *The Doors*. Here, Densmore plays a generic bossa nova pattern. This bossa nova pattern is shown in Figure 12-12. Like the previous pattern, a cross stick is implemented and you will ride on the cymbal. Also like the previous pattern, you will chick quarter notes

FIGURE 12-11:
"The End"
basic idea

c. ♩=104

Use a cross stick on the rim of the snare (beat 4).
Also, turn the snares *off* for this song.

Note: This is NOT an actual transcription.

FIGURE 12-12:
"Break On Through" bossa nova idea

c. ♩=188

Use a cross stick on the rim of the snare!

This is a universal beat used in bossa nova music.

in the hi-hat foot. This beat uses a 3 + 2 clave rhythm, which is universal in Latin music. The 3 represents the three rim clicks you play in measure one; the 2 represents the two rim clicks you will play in measure two.

Mitch Mitchell

Mitch Mitchell (born 1947) is best known for his work with Jimi Hendrix. Like many others, jazz drummers Elvin Jones and Art Blakey played a pivotal role in this British drummer's development. Mitchell's style was both elegant and raw, and like Keith Moon, his extroverted approach pushed the drums into the spotlight. Mitchell's method of drumming worked well with Hendrix's music since it was highly improvisational, bluesy, psychedelic, and jam oriented. It was the perfect setting for a creative—albeit note-y—drummer like Mitchell.

Figure 12-13 shows the underlying groove Mitchell plays during the verses of "Purple Haze" from *Are You Experienced*. This is merely the basic pattern over which Mitchell improvises. In other words, think of this beat as the idea behind Mitchell's improvisations. Indeed, Mitchell does use variations at will. For example, he uses different surfaces (snare and tom-toms) each time he plays the sixteenth-note fill seen in the second measure. Later, he swaps this lick out altogether in favor of a sextuplet fill. (He was very fond of sextuplets in general.)

On another classic track, "Fire" from *Are You Experienced,* Mitchell plays both a solid, rocking groove and a cornucopia of tasty fills. Twice he also plays a groove variation that is particularly funky. Figure 12-14 illuminates the basic idea behind Mitchell's groove variation. Be sure to check out Mitchell's

FIGURE 12-13:
"Purple Haze"
idea

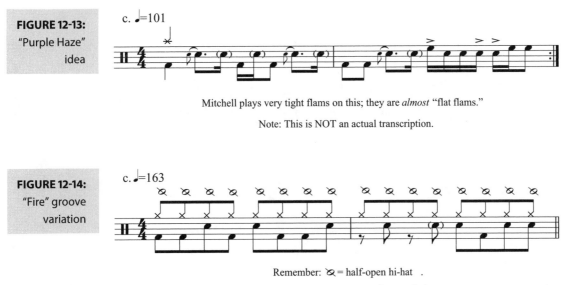

Mitchell plays very tight flams on this; they are *almost* "flat flams."

Note: This is NOT an actual transcription.

FIGURE 12-14:
"Fire" groove
variation

Remember: ⊗ = half-open hi-hat .

Note: This is NOT an actual transcription.

entire performance on this tune—it is a classic among classics. Additionally, you should familiarize yourself with all three legendary Jimi Hendrix Experience studio albums: *Are You Experienced, Axis: Bold as Love,* and *Electric Ladyland.*

Keith Moon

Keith Moon (1946–1978) is another iconic figure in rock. The drummer for The Who, Moon was an eccentric character whose playing style reflected his energetic, frenetic personality. Known for odd behavior and heavy substance abuse, Moon earned the nickname "Moon the Loon" during his many years with The Who. Unfortunately, Moon's lunacy and self-destructive lifestyle caught up with him, and he died from a drug overdose in 1978 at the age of thirty-two.

As a drummer, Moon was like no one else. Contemporaries John Densmore and Mitch Mitchell played with freewheeling spirits, but compared to Moon's maniacal bashing, these drummers seemed polite. Moon was often criticized for soloing over the entire song. In truth, he did hunker down

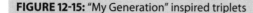

FIGURE 12-15: "My Generation" inspired triplets

Track 54

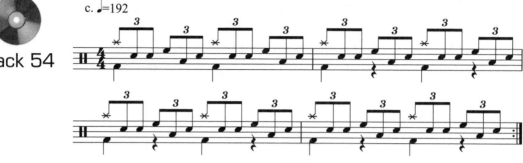

Alternate and begin with the right hand.

and play deep grooves when the music required it. However, Moon's playing always seemed to be in a perpetual climax. He certainly had an inexhaustible cache of fills to pull from and he would often ride wildly on his crash cymbals. All this created a frenzied sound. However, this approach infused The Who's music with beautiful abandon and Moon's playing won over most listeners immediately. On the ending to "My Generation," from the album of the same name, you will hear Moon's over-the-top style. Here, he plays eighth-note triplets around his kit. He crashes on beats one and three. In between, he moves his sticks around the snare and tom-toms. Moon-inspired triplets are shown to you in Figure 12-15. As with many of these figures, this figure merely captures the essence of Moon's fills. It is not a literal transcription.

Moon's ride pattern on "Baba O Riley" from the album *Who's Next* (1971) represents this drummer's overall approach to keeping time. As mentioned earlier, Moon's tendency was to ride on his cymbals like crashes. Moon wasn't the only drummer to ride in this manner, but his version of "crash riding" had the drive and momentum of a Mack truck, which is one of the reasons his drumming is so exciting. Figure 12-16 shows some "Baba O Riley" variations. These are beat options. Moon changes things up almost randomly; therefore, Figure 12-16 shows you only the idea behind his improvisations.

FIGURE 12-16:

"Baba O Riley" basic idea with variations

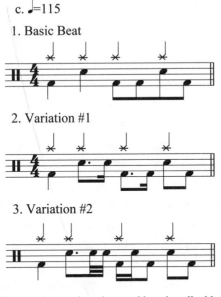

c. ♩=115

1. Basic Beat

2. Variation #1

3. Variation #2

These are beat options that would work well with the overall *feel* of this song.

Note: This is NOT an actual transcription.

Ginger Baker

This chapter would not be complete without a discussion of Ginger Baker (born 1939). Baker is a British innovator, best known for his work with the blues-rock bands Cream and Blind Faith. A lifelong devotee to jazz, Baker has also made forays into this realm with his own trio featuring Bill Frisell on guitar and Charlie Haden on bass.

Although some reunions have taken place, Cream was a short-lived band (1966–1968) and Blind Faith was even shorter lived (one album). Despite this, Baker's contributions are manifold. His work with Cream is particularly legendary. Ginger Baker was the unofficial founder of this band and his drumming was often featured in their music. Sometimes Cream songs were more structured and tuneful; other times, they were nothing more than long psychedelic jams. The album *Disraeli Gears* is the band's greatest commercial success. This LP yielded two rock classics, "Strange Brew" and "Sunshine of Your Love." The latter featured a Native American inspired drumbeat by Baker, which is a simulation of powwow drumming. Baker's basic idea is shown in Figure 12-17. This is a simple pattern that is actually rather generic; nonetheless, it works beautifully on this song.

The jam song "Toad" was Baker's solo feature. It also holds the distinction of being one of the first extended drum solos in rock. This piece was first heard on 1966's *Fresh Cream*. Moreover, a live version was tagged on to the end of 1968's *Wheels of Fire*. On both solos, Baker develops his ideas gradually but with great intensity. For some listeners, his solos may linger on too long. For others, they are the pinnacles of drum composition because they sound composed, even though they are improvised.

Either way, it seems hard to imagine 1970s icons like Bill Bruford, Carl Palmer, John Bonham, and Neil Peart were not being influenced—at least indirectly—by Baker's advanced soloing concepts. In truth, Baker was one of the first drummers to fuse rudimental and jazzy elements together in a loud rock setting. Like Keith Moon, he was also an early proponent of double bass drums, a concept you will learn more about in the next two chapters.

FIGURE 12-17:
"Sunshine of Your Love" basic beat

Note: This is NOT an actual transcription.

Chapter 13

Hard Rock and Heavy Metal

Hard rock and heavy metal are two essential substyles of rock music. In this chapter, you will get a sense for both styles by focusing on the most important groups in these genres. First, you will learn about John Bonham, whose influence is peerless in both hard rock and metal. Next, you will learn about Nicko McBrain, arguably the finest "classic" heavy metal drummer. After this, you will explore the style of Lars Ulrich, a modern master of "thrash metal." Last, you will be introduced to double bass drum techniques.

John Henry Bonham

It wouldn't be a stretch to call John Bonham (1948–1980) one of the greatest drummers ever. In the minds of many contemporary players, this is a fact. Without a doubt, Bonham is among the most revered drummers in rock. There is something unbelievable and wholly infectious about this British drummer's playing. And indeed, this "something" is difficult to pin down. Bonham was the ultimate groove master, and yet he was also a fantastic soloist. At once, Bonham supported and stole the spotlight. Few drummers can ride two roads at the same time like Bonham did; for this, he is quite unique and special.

John Bonham's feel is a vital part of his drumming. This feel has been copied by hundreds of drummers over the years. In fact, it's hard to say what such diverse players as Abe Laboriel Jr., Cindy Blackman, Alex Van Halen, Joey Kramer, and other heavy-hitting drummers would sound like today if Bonham had never existed.

Bonham almost single-handedly ushered in a whole new approach to the instrument. Before Bonham, there were loud drummers, but not necessarily "heavy hitters." Bonham used his arms in a whipping motion to generate a sound on his kit that many drummers have since co-opted. Bonham used large Paiste cymbals and deep Ludwig drums plus practically tree-trunk-size drumsticks. This allowed him to create a larger than life sound, one that could cut through stacks of speaker cabinets in stadiums.

Formed in 1968, Led Zeppelin made eight studio albums and one documentary film, entitled *The Song Remains the Same*. Other materials have been released posthumously. During their twelve-year span (1968–1980), Led Zeppelin wrote and recorded countless rock hits. Among them are "Good Times Bad Times," "Communication Breakdown," "Immigrant Song," "Black Dog," "Ramble On," "Rock and Roll," "Kashmir," and arguably the most famous rock anthem of all time, "Stairway to Heaven."

Bonham also played a famous drum solo on the track "Moby Dick." This song was first heard on the album *Led Zeppelin II*. Many versions of this solo have surfaced over the years. On the 2003 DVD entitled *Led Zeppelin,* fans are treated to a version of "Moby Dick" from a 1970 Royal Albert Hall concert. Here, Bonham's solo begins by quoting Max Roach's "The Drum also Waltzes." The solo then undergoes many developments and shifts, including an interlude where Bonham plays drums with his bare hands.

The solo clearly borrows from the showmanship of jazz drummers Gene Krupa and Buddy Rich, and the more melodic nuances of Joe Morello and Max Roach. However, the through-composed, long-form nature of the solo likely derives from Ginger Baker's solo performance on "The Toad."

Unfortunately, the world never saw Bonham's artistry fully bloom. One gets the feeling that this drummer still had a lot of music, ideas, and growth left in him despite his extraordinary accomplishments with Led Zeppelin. However, in 1980, Bonham's life was cut short due to an alcohol overdose. Like Keith Moon, Bonham was silenced at age thirty-two.

Playing in the Style of John Bonham

Many publications are dedicated to an analysis of John Bonham's playing. This book will get you thinking about the way he approached music. In other words, you will study his ideas rather than note-for-note transcriptions. First, go back and review Figure 7-5, where you learned how to play beats using sixteenth-note triplets in the bass drum. On "Good Times Bad Times" (from the album *Led Zeppelin*), Bonham uses these types of patterns often.

Also be sure to review Figures 8-9 and 9-7, and apply these patterns to soloing. In these figures, you will see sixteenth notes and sixteenth-note triplets (sextuplets) broken up between the hands and the bass drum. Pattern number 2 from Figure 8-9 is especially Bonham oriented, as are all five patterns from Figure 9-7.

Figure 13-1 shows you the basic idea or rhythmical template behind "Immigrant Song," from *Led Zeppelin III.* Listen to Bonham's performance on this tune. You will hear how thunderous his playing can be.

Bonham plays an equally fat beat on the cover of "When the Levee Breaks," from *Led Zeppelin IV.* On this song, Bonham's playing is as solid as a rock. His basic idea is shown to you in Figure 13-2.

FIGURE 13-1:
"Immigrant Song" basic idea

Note: This is NOT an actual transcription.

FIGURE 13-2:
"When the Levee Breaks" basic idea

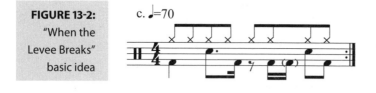

Note: This is NOT an actual transcription.

On "Whole Lotta Love," from the album *Led Zeppelin II*, Bonham plays yet another deep-pocketed groove that couldn't be funkier or more impressive. This basic rhythmical idea is shown in Figure 13-3. On top of this groove, Bonham improvises ad lib.

FIGURE 13-3:
"Whole Lotta Love" basic idea.

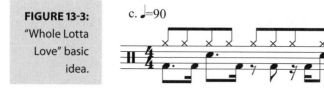

Note: This is NOT an actual transcription.

On "Whole Lotta Love," Bonham also plays fills that employ sixteenth notes, sextuplets, and eighth-note triplets. He also uses combinations of sixteenth notes and sextuplets or sextuplets and eighth-note triplets. These combinations of notes make fills feel elastic, as if they're stretching out. Try this idea when you fill in rock music. It's a neat effect and not very difficult to achieve, as long as you are careful to play in time and are rhythmically accurate. Four "Whole Lotta Love" inspired fills are notated in Figure 13-4.

On "The Crunge," from *Houses of the Holy,* Bonham plays a syncopated, odd metered beat on the verses. He also employs tricky open hi-hats. The beat could be written in 9/4, but for conceptual reasons, it's easier to feel this beat in the mixed meter 5/4 + 4/4. As you play this beat, be very careful of the open hi-hats. On the actual recording, notice how Bonham does not strike the

FIGURE 13-4: "Whole Lotta Love"-inspired fills

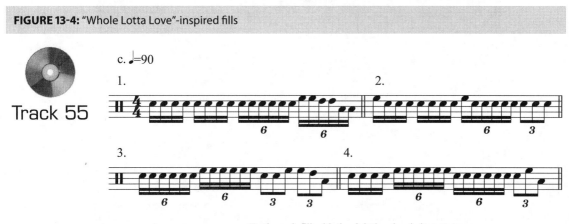

Track 55

Begin each fill with the right hand and alternate!

hi-hat on the closed (+) note. The closed notes are played only with the hi-hat foot. The rhythmical underpinning of "The Crunge" is shown in Figure 13-5.

On the introduction to "Rock and Roll," from *Led Zeppelin IV,* Bonham plays only half-open hi-hat and snare drum (no bass drum). Here, Bonham plays four measures of 4/4 time together with three pickup notes. In addition to the studio version, be sure to check out this song on the live album, *How the West Was Won* (released 2003). See Figure 13-6 for an example of what Bonham might play for this introduction if he were to experiment with shifting accents between the snare and hi-hat.

Bonham plays a snare drum beat on "Gallows Pole," from *Led Zeppelin III,* that suggests New Orleans second-line drumming, though whether this is intentional or not cannot be proved. Nonetheless, the syncopated snare drum pattern Bonham uses is reminiscent of second line's traditional, marching style of snare drumming. Certainly, Bonham could very well have been exposed to New Orleans music given this band's obsession with American blues. The underlying rhythmical idea used by Bonham is shown in Figure 13-7. Throughout the song, he improvises over this motif.

FIGURE 13-5:
"The Crunge" basic idea

Be careful of the open hi-hats!

Note: This is NOT an actual transcription.

FIGURE 13-6:
"Rock and Roll" intro idea

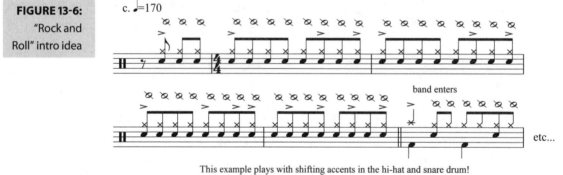

This example plays with shifting accents in the hi-hat and snare drum!
Note: This is NOT an actual transcription.

FIGURE 13-7:
"Gallows Pole" snare drum idea

Play the unaccented notes on the snare drum softly!

Note: This is NOT an actual transcription.

Classic Heavy Metal and Nicko McBrain

In a nutshell, hard rock bands such as Led Zeppelin, Deep Purple, and Steppenwolf paved the way for the rise of heavy metal. As discussed in Chapter 1, heavy metal is an extreme version of hard rock. It was first developed in the UK in the 1970s but has since become an international phenomenon. Various forms of metal are still popular today, especially among young white males.

The most important classic heavy metal bands are Black Sabbath, Judas Priest, Motorhead, and Iron Maiden. All of these bands hail from Great Britain, and they all had an impact on modern heavy metal, even though they now seem tame compared to newer (and harsher) incarnations of metal such as speed metal and death metal.

Iron Maiden's album *Piece of Mind* is the first album to feature drummer Nicko McBrain (born 1954), as previous drummer, Clive Burr, left after *The Number of the Beast* tour. McBrain's style is unique in heavy metal. First, he is one of the few to avoid a double bass drum or double pedal. (In the studio, he used a double pedal on one song but quickly discarded it and he has only used it rarely in live settings.) Second, McBrain's ability to rhythmically match complex, linear bass and guitar lines underscores his considerable technique. Bassist and songwriter Steve Harris has often commented on McBrain's ability to riff along with the guitars in a close note-for-note fashion.

FACT

Like most rock drummers of his generation, Nicko McBrain was influenced first by jazz drummers. He has cited Joe Morello as his earliest inspiration. Morello was a technical master, not unlike Buddy Rich, and his solo on Dave Brubeck's "Take Five" has long been considered a watershed moment in drumming.

Despite his interest in jazz, it wouldn't be long before the rock star bug bit McBrain. Much of this was due to The Beatles. As a kid, McBrain was obsessed with Ringo Starr and longed to be just like him.

McBrain's desire to be a rock star was granted when he joined Iron Maiden in 1983. Even early on, McBrain's drumming was a prominent feature in Iron Maiden's music. His ride cymbal work is particularly impressive on *Piece of Mind*. This is best evidenced on the songs, "Where Eagles Dare," and "Quest for Fire." The basic beats for these tunes are shown in Figures 13-8 and 13-9, respectively. The beats in these figures show you only the rhythmical idea behind each groove; the recording itself reveals far more intricacies and variations.

"Where Eagles Dare" and "Quest for Fire" are in 6/8 time. This means that the eighth note gets or receives one beat, and there are six eighth notes in one measure. Often, this meter is counted in two. Like 12/8, the dotted quarter note is felt as its pulse.

One fill that McBrain uses often incorporates the four-stroke ruff. This is a standard rudiment that uses three grace notes and one main note. The four-stroke ruff has many applications on the drum set, and you can experiment with several different stickings. However, the most common way to play this rudiment is with a single-stroke sticking. Traditionally, the snare drummer begins with the left hand. Figure 13-10 shows you the four-stroke ruff (A) followed by two drum-set applications (B and C). You will see the

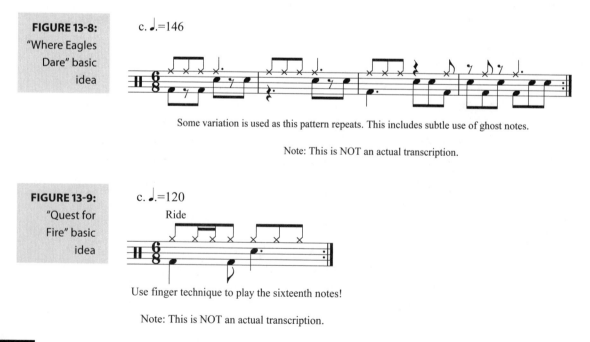

FIGURE 13-8: "Where Eagles Dare" basic idea

c. ♩.=146

Some variation is used as this pattern repeats. This includes subtle use of ghost notes.

Note: This is NOT an actual transcription.

FIGURE 13-9: "Quest for Fire" basic idea

c. ♩.=120

Ride

Use finger technique to play the sixteenth notes!

Note: This is NOT an actual transcription.

pattern broken up between the hands and the bass drum foot. Here, the bass drum plays the main note, while the hands play the grace notes. Jazz drummers were the first to use this lick. It is typically used as a sharp musical period or "thump."

FIGURE 13-10: Four-stroke ruff as a rudiment and around the kit

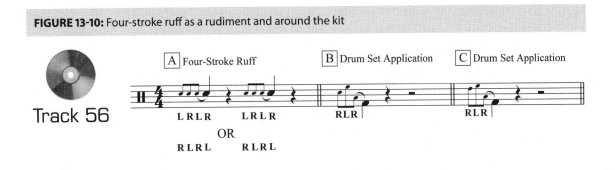

Track 56

American Heavy Metal and Lars Ulrich

Along with Megadeth, Anthrax, and Slayer, Metallica spearheaded one of the most popular substyles of heavy metal, called thrash metal. However, as the band matured, they entered into the mainstream with a self-titled album that has since been referred to as *The Black Album*. This record, while still heavy hitting, featured such hits as "Nothing Else Matters" and the very popular "Enter Sandman."

Drummer Lars Ulrich (born 1963) was the cofounder of Metallica, and his percussive skills remain a focal point of the group's sound. Ulrich was born in Denmark and moved to the United States to pursue a career in tennis, but instead found himself drawn to music and drumming. Ulrich's musical inspiration came when he saw Ian Paice play with Deep Purple, and the seeds were sown for a career in rock at age thirteen when Ulrich received his first Ludwig drum kit from his parents. At age eighteen, the young Ulrich met singer James Hetfield, they formed Metallica, and the rest is history. To date, Metallica has sold over 90 million record albums internationally.

As a drummer, Ulrich's style may be the very definition of modern heavy drumming. Unlike the heavy hitting of John Bonham, Ulrich's approach is more precise and exacting. This is not to say that Bonham's drumming was loose. Ulrich's playing, however, is particularly ironclad and metronomic.

These qualities are key characteristics in thrash metal. For example, double bass-drum flourishes sound like machine guns and tom-tom beats almost sound computerized.

With some exceptions, Ulrich's style is decidedly inorganic, though it contains all the passion and intensity you would ever want from a drummer. The inorganic element comes from Ulrich's lack of warm, earthy jazzy influences. (This contrasts with hard rock and classic metal drummers such as Bonham and McBrain, respectively.) Because he is not building off of drummers like Joe Morello, Elvin Jones, or Art Blakey, he does not employ a lot of finesse. He also rarely creates subtle colors on his drums and cymbals. But this is not a criticism of Ulrich's playing.

Thrash metal is not *supposed* to groove like a swampy N'awlin's march or seethe like a James Brown funk vamp. Nor is it supposed to swing or contain understated cymbal textures and dark earth tones. The beauty of Ulrich's playing lies in its pure unbridled power. Metallica's music is a concentrated and mind-blowing musical assault. There is great bombast and energy in their music and, again, it's *supposed* to strike the listeners this way.

Ulrich's style of drumming is also extremely difficult to play. In truth, few drummers can do it well. Most who attempt to play like Ulrich sound sloppy and, frankly, out of breath; they just don't have the dexterity. Ulrich, on the other hand, is impressive to listen to (and watch) if only because he has great stamina and such overwhelming musical drive. He remains one of the most significant heavy metal innovators.

Single Bass Drum Versus Double Bass Drums

Lars Ulrich, Charlie Benante (Anthrax), and Dave Lombardo (Slayer) are the most important thrash metal drummers. They also all use double kick very effectively. However, playing double bass drums (or double pedal) is not as easy as it sounds. In fact, it's quite difficult, especially if you have little experience using your hi-hat foot. Therefore, if you wish to use two bass drums, the first step is to strengthen your hi-hat foot. How do you do this? Practice implementing various hi-hat foot ostinatos when playing beat, fills, and solos.

As an amateur, you should be careful not to rely on your second bass drum too much, or you will never develop solid technique in your main bass drum foot. In general, if you lean on double-kick drumming too much, it will become a crutch. Don't forget, Lars Ulrich is a great single bass drummer first. He uses his double bass drums often; however, they are used for musical and conceptual reason. He doesn't use double bass drums because he doesn't know how to play with a single bass drum. In the end, if you don't know how to play well with just a single pedal, you should avoid using a double pedal or double bass drums.

FACT

American drummer Tommy Aldridge (born 1950) is one of the world's finest double bass drummers. Influenced by John Bonham and modern jazz drummers, Aldridge has performed with Ozzy Osborne, Whitesnake, and Ted Nugent, among others. One of the first to play double kick with astonishing speed and power, Aldridge continues to wow audiences with his phenomenal technique.

After you've developed some identifiable skill with one pedal, then and only then, experiment with a double pedal or double bass drums. If double-bass drumming is not for you, that's okay, too. As previously mentioned, Nicko McBrain doesn't use one. Also, John Bonham and Buddy Rich never used one. But you wouldn't know it given the fast, thunderous bass-drum playing displayed by all these players.

Double Bass Drum Patterns

The patterns in Figure 13-11 show you some double bass drum grooves, which are commonly used by heavy metal drummers. While you can use a heel's-down technique on these, it's best to play on the ball of your foot using a heel's-up approach. When you use the heel's-up method, you will be able to play louder. More than anything, these beats must be played very accurately and with a lot of power and energy. Otherwise, you will not evoke the true spirit and feel of heavy metal drumming.

As noted in the figure, you should use your ride cymbal as your ride surface. When playing double pedal, your hi-hat is effectively out of commission because you cannot create a closed sound for riding. However, some drummers who use double kicks add auxiliary hi-hats to their setups. This is an additional hi-hat arm containing two loosely clamped-together hi-hat cymbals. It's usually set up on the right side of the kit like a ride cymbal.

The patterns in Figure 13-11 use a variety of rhythms. Examples 1 and 2 utilize eighth notes. Example number 2 is also written in 2/2, or cut time. This means that the half note gets or receives one beat and there are two half notes per measure. (In this meter, quarter notes act like eighth notes.) In music, 2/2 is only used for up tempos, so play number 2 fast. Pattern numbers 3, 4, and 5 explore sixteenth notes and eighth-sixteenth combinations. These rhythmical groupings should be very familiar to you now. Pattern numbers 6 and 7 move into eighth-note triplets; the latter creates a shuffle feel, and predictably, pattern numbers 8 and 9 employ sextuplets. Again, the latter is a fast shuffle rhythm. Pattern numbers 10 and 11 use thirty-second notes. These examples will be the most difficult to play because the notes fly by so quickly. Remember: precision, power, speed, and stamina. These are key elements of double bass drumming and heavy metal music.

FIGURE 13-11: Beats using double bass drums

Track 57

Use the ride cymbal for all of these beats. Alternately, you may use an auxiliary hi-hat.

Pattern #'s 1, 3, 7, and 10 are played on the CD.

Chapter 14
Neil Peart and Drum Composition

This chapter is dedicated to Neil Peart and drum composition. One of rock's finest drummers, Peart made it cool to be smart, literate, and analytical behind the kit. His influence on up-and-coming rock drummers spans three generations, and his status as a music icon only continues to grow. Students of rock drumming should study Peart's music and philosophy because he represents both the old school, or roots, of drumming and the tech-driven, modern age of drum set performance.

Neil Peart

Neil Peart was born on a farm outside of Hamilton, Ontario, in 1952. Growing up in nearby Port Dalhousie, Peart was first exposed to music through compulsory piano lessons, which he detested. At age thirteen, he began playing the drums, but only on a practice pad. Soon, however, he got his first drum set (a three-piece Stewart), and he began studying in earnest. Like most young drummers, Peart cut his teeth playing with local bands, which no doubt showcased his burgeoning talents.

Seeking more, at age eighteen, Peart moved to London, England, to pursue an international career as a drummer. However, a year and a half later, the disappointed young Peart moved back to Canada, where he put his ambitions on hold. But as luck would have it, in 1974, he was invited to audition for the Toronto band called Rush. As a member of Rush, Peart would go on to sell millions of records worldwide, mount massive world tours, become inducted into the Modern Drummer Hall of Fame, and receive the Order of Canada, the country's most esteemed civilian honor.

FACT

Nicknamed "the professor," Neal Peart is an established author, having written four nonfiction books (as of this publication). His books have sold over 100,000 copies and he was nominated for a Canadian Literary Award in 2003. He also writes all the song lyrics for Rush, and according to his books, is an avid bicycle, motorcycle, and travel enthusiast.

Like all of the drummers discussed in this book, it would be impossible to sum up the extensive career of Peart with just a few pages of text and a handful of musical examples. Therefore, an attempt has been made to expose you only to key points and essentials as they relate to the goals of this book. It's up to you to conduct your own research so you may gain a more comprehensive picture of this drummer and his music.

Composing Drum Parts

In an online essay about the 2007 Rush album *Snakes and Arrows,* Peart states, "As a drummer, it has become apparent to me that I am more of a 'composer' than an 'improviser.'" This isn't to say that Peart doesn't improvise; he does. However, his inclination is to devise exact parts, and then play them with the precision of a classical percussionist.

His process for creating drum compositions is explained in great detail in the DVD *A Work in Progress.* This educational video documents Peart's development as a drummer with specific references made to the 1996 Rush release *Test for Echo.* Peart extols his creative process then provides musical examples to support his methods. Additionally, he talks at length about his technical approach to the instrument. If all this sounds scholarly, it is. Peart has a strong inclination toward complex analysis. However, to make things user friendly, the professor includes slowed-down audio and video so viewers may follow the musical examples more comprehensibly.

What does drum composition mean for you? If you play in a band, you will likely want to create drum parts that go beyond simplistic beats or free improvisation. Peart's approach begins with the structure of a song. He thinks about how the drums might highlight each section or portion of the music. In other words, he writes drum parts that complement the other instruments and singer, Geddy Lee. For example, Peart might choose subdued, darker textures for the verses and explosive, brighter colors on the choruses, creating contrast and forward momentum at each turn. However, this is by no means a formula. On another song, his approach may be totally different; it all depends on the character and feel of the music. Each song has its own distinct personality, and Peart writes drum parts with this in mind.

Song Sections

Because Rush plays what might be termed "hard prog-rock," their songs tend to have intricate parts, interludes, and diversions. Therefore, Peart is usually blending together several colors and textures in an attempt to meet the needs of a large quantity of song sections. However, most drummers play music that is less involved. Likely, you will not need to grapple with so many song parts, unless you play in a prog-rock or art rock ensemble. For example, classic rock and pop music can still be quirky, but it doesn't require the drummer to make so many textural shifts in a single song. And this is good news for just learning how to create drum parts.

Never thought of drum set playing as compositional? Even though drums and cymbals are indefinite pitched instruments, they still have the ability to tell an elegant musical story. Neil Peart's extended drum solos are popular because he carefully weaves a tale through rhythmical, melodic, and harmonic development. You don't need specific pitches—like C or B-flat—to convey these musical elements. You do, however, need musical organization and a well-founded structure.

For Peart, each song section gets a slightly different treatment, though he also smartly uses repetition in his playing. Repetition helps ward off compositional mishmashes and part-writing incongruities. (Repetition is also logical since virtually all song arrangements contain sections that repeat, recapitulate, or both.) Overall, when you write drum parts, you should think about the different surfaces of your kit—drums, cymbals, auxiliary percussion, etc.—as colors and textures. Your job is to create a musical painting that can be used to accompany the sounds being made by your fellow band mates.

Playing in the Style of Neil Peart

It's time to explore the ideas behind a variety of Rush drum parts. Unfortunately, there is not enough space in this book to delve deeply into the decision-making process behind each idea. However, this is okay because, by now, you should trust your own musical instincts. The first example draws from Rush's 1978 album *Hemispheres*. The song is "La Villa Strangiato." On this tune, Peart plays some really creative beats and some equally fantastic drum breaks. Figure 14-1 shows you the basic idea behind a hi-hat beat that appears in this epic song. Here, the open hi-hats come and go quickly, so be sure to practice the intricate pedaling on this.

FIGURE 14-1:
"La Villa Strangiato" hi-hat idea

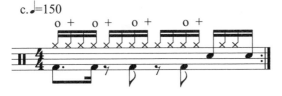

Note: This is NOT an actual transcription.

On "La Villa Strangiato," Peart also plays one of his many trademark ride variations. Figure 14-2 breaks up paradiddles between the hands on the bell of the cymbal and the snare drum. This is the underlying beat for this section in the tune. However, bear in mind that Peart adds bass drum variations throughout in an ad-lib fashion. This beat is included here to show you the universal applications of paradiddles.

FIGURE 14-2:
"La Villa Strangiato" ride cymbal idea

Note: This is NOT an actual transcription.

Peart plays a similar ride pattern on "YYZ," an instrumental track off of 1981's *Moving Pictures*. Here, the bass drum is a little more active. Again, though, the kick drum pattern is sometimes altered. Often, in the beginning of phrases, Peart omits the two sixteenth notes or the "+ ah" of beat one.

This ride pattern is also something of a Peart cliché. For example, you will hear the same beat used in "The Spirit of Radio" from 1980's *Permanent Waves*. Again, the notation shown here is the underlying rhythmical model, which is then used to create all kinds of interesting variations.

FIGURE 14-3:
"YYZ" ride cymbal idea

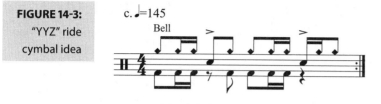

Note: This is NOT an actual transcription.

Odd Time-Signatures

Rush is known for its extensive use of odd time-signatures. This is, no doubt, the progressive aspect of their repertoire. For example, "YYZ" begins with a motif in 5/8. Peart first plays it on a tiny cymbal. While it's difficult to say exactly what type of cymbal he's using for this, it's probably a generic "bell" of some sort. This motif is outlined in Figure 14-4.

FIGURE 14-4:
"YYZ" motif

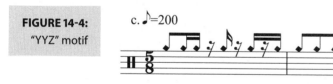

After the intro, Peart orchestrates the 5/8 motif around the kit first between the hi-hat, snare, and bass drum, then between the snare, bass drum, and ride cymbal. He uses a transitional fill in between each phrase. One hi-hat, snare, and bass drum variation is shown in Figure 14-5. Be mindful of the half-open hi-hat notes here, and recognize that this pattern can have other variations (as heard on live recordings such as *Exit...Stage Left* and *Rush in Rio.*) Like all of the other examples in this chapter, think of the notation in Figure 14-5 as a basic template.

FIGURE 14-5:
"YYZ" hi-hat, snare, and bass drum variation for drum set

c. ♪=200

Note: This is NOT an actual transcription.

Other songs, such as "Tom Sawyer," from the album *Moving Pictures*, use odd time-signatures. On this song, Peart plays a beat in 7/4, riding first on the hi-hat during the synthesizer melody, and then on the ride cymbal for the guitar solo. His 7/4 hi-hat beat has some interesting open hi-hat syncopations. Figure 14-6 shows a spinoff from Peart's performance on the live album *Exit...Stage Left*.

FIGURE 14-6:
Hi-hat beat spin-off from "Tom Sawyer"

c. ♩=185

If you listen to "Free Will," from the album *Permanent Waves*, you will hear mixed meters being used. Mixed meters means that you will toggle back and forth between time signatures. In "Free Will," the introduction alternates between 6/4 and 7/4 time. The groove illustrated in Figure 14-7 is reminiscent of Peart's beat from *Exit...Stage Left*.

FIGURE 14-7:
"Free Will" mixed-meter idea

c. ♩=160
Ride

Note: This is NOT an actual transcription.

As if this wasn't difficult enough, the verses to "Free Will" shift meter constantly. Figure 14-8 illustrates the meter changes for the verse of "Free Will" in a rhythmic spin-off. Play the sixteenth notes in the 9/4 measure using double lefts (LL).

FIGURE 14-8:
"Free Will"
verse
structure
spin-off

Note: This is NOT an actual transcription.

Neil Peart's Fills

In general, Peart's fills are largely based around sixteenth notes, thirty-second notes, and triplets. Sometimes he plays includes sextuplets on beat four of the measure. Figure 14-9 shows you this fill. He plays this pattern twice on "Roll the Bones," from the album of the same name. Sometimes Peart will add tom-toms. Other times, he plays it on the snare drum only. He also may extend it, playing sextuplets over beats three and four. Further, he might play sextuplets over the whole measure or end them on beat four, etc.

In truth, there are lots of ways to use and vary sextuplets, and you should have already explored some sextuplet applications earlier in this book. Check out Peart's performance on "Summertime Blues" from *Feedback*. On this tune, he plays two well-placed sextuplet fills that are reminiscent of Keith Moon's freewheeling style (see Chapter 12). Sextuplet fills are

FIGURE 14-9:
Sextuplet fill

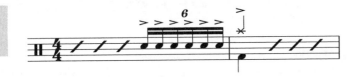

common, indeed universal, to rock drumming. You can also hear these fills played by dozens of other drummers on scores of other songs.

More than anything, Peart is known for linear fills around his tom-toms. These fills usually move from high to low across many drums. (His setup from the 2007 *Snakes and Arrows* tour boasted eight tom-toms.) Since this book is tailored to a five-piece kit, you cannot get the full melodic effect of Peart's fills. However, you can simulate them. Figure 14-10 shows you some Peart-inspired fills using thirty-second notes with sixteenths. Play these fills using single-stroke stickings. You may lead off with either hand.

The Influence of Buddy Rich

Fans of Neil Peart have come to expect a drum solo at every concert. True to form, each Rush tour boasts a newly composed solo, though Peart does rework and revise previous ideas and themes. Particularly inspired solos are heard on *Exit...Stage Left, A Show of Hands,* and *Different Stages.* The 2003 live album, *Rush in Rio,* features a through-composed solo called "O Baterista." This solo includes a surprise "duet" between Peart and The Buddy

FIGURE 14-10: Neil Peart-inspired fills written for a five-piece kit

Track 58

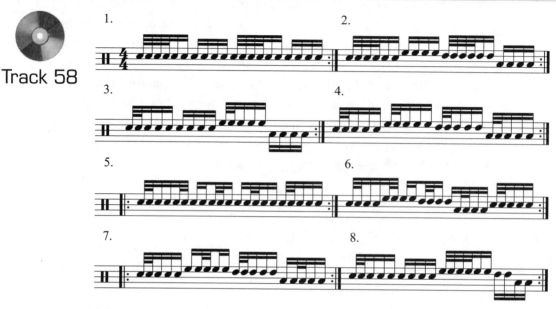

Pattern #'s 1, 4, and 8 are played on the CD.

Rich Orchestra (via recording). In other words, for his solo's climax, Peart plays along with a recorded version of the shout chorus from "One O'Clock Jump." This ending is a heartfelt homage to the big-band era and the inimitable Rich himself.

ESSENTIAL

In the 1990s, Neil Peart produced two albums featuring many of the world's finest rock and jazz drummers performing with the Buddy Rich Orchestra. Peart himself plays on the jazz standards "One O'clock Jump" and "Cotton Tail." Aptly named *Burning for Buddy,* these recordings were released in two volumes. Rich died in 1987 at the age of sixty-nine.

Buddy Rich was a wunderkind. In fact, he was playing drums as "Traps the Boy Wonder" in Vaudevillian acts as young as eighteen months old. He never took drum lessons or even practiced. However, many consider him to be the best drummer that ever lived. Without a doubt, Rich possessed unparalleled technique, limb independence, and, most of all, speed, speed, and more speed! Even the finest drummers today must use sustained, intense practice to approximate the speed and stick control of Rich.

Rich became known primarily as a bandleader, but he also worked as a sideman for decades. Among others, Rich had three notable stints with the Tommy Dorsey Orchestra. He also worked with Harry James off and on throughout the 1950s and 1960s. Throughout the '60s, '70s, and '80s, Johnny Carson, host of *The Tonight Show,* often featured Rich on his television program. These TV appearances catapulted Rich's career into the mainstream, where he enjoyed "household name" celebrity status.

Few serious drummers could say Rich hasn't influenced them in some way; his musical impact is simply too great. It has been said that the great jazz drummer Elvin Jones once remarked, "He [Rich] can't be denied." Whether this quote is apocryphal or not, you'd be hard pressed to find any serious drummer who would disagree with this sentiment.

Any time you see a drummer playing rudimental snare drum patterns, he or she is probably invoking the spirit of Buddy Rich and other swing-era drummers. These other drummers include Gene Krupa, Chick Webb, Ray McKinley, Joe Jones, Warren "Baby" Dodds, and Big Sid Catlett. These drummers were all great. However, none of them could solo with the same technical wizardry as Buddy Rich. He is, and will always be, one of the most exciting soloists in percussive history.

FACT

Because of his dedication to self-improvement, Neil Peart continues to grow and perfect his craft. In the 1990s, after thirty years of professional playing, Peart revamped his entire approach to the instrument. To do this, he studied under legendary teacher and mentor Freddie Gruber, who was a close associate of Buddy Rich's. Gruber's methods are based on keen observations of Rich.

If you listen to Neil Peart's solo "O Baterista," from the album *Rush in Rio,* there are distinct sections that feature rudimental playing. For example, the solo's opening is very rudimental. A spinoff of the first four measures of Peart's solo is shown in Figure 14-11. This is not an actual transcription. Instead, it's a rudimental solo excerpt inspired by Peart's playing. You will see a lot of syncopation, ghost notes, and seven-stroke rolls. The old timers were very partial to the snare drum and snare drum soloing. In the 1940s, tom-toms were often used only for accents. Peart's use of the snare drum—almost exclusively—in the opening of his solo is no accident. Again, he's invoking the spirit of swing-era drumming, and most of all, Buddy Rich.

If you wish to delve deeper into rudimental drum set soloing, be sure to see Figure 10-4 found earlier in this book. Also, be sure to check out Peart's 2005 video, *Anatomy of a Drum Solo*. In this DVD, he breaks down "O Baterista" (renamed "Der Trommler") into several distinct sections or elements. He also explains the ideas and concepts behind each mini movement. If you're interested in learning how to blend old-school rudimental approaches with modern rock, this DVD is a must have.

Technique Builders for Double Bass Drum

You first learned about double bass drum patterns in Chapter 13. Now it's time to take your knowledge a step further by building technique between the feet and the hands for use in solos. Neil Peart, like many drummers today, is an excellent double bass drummer. Like other double kick or dou-

FIGURE 14-11:
"O Baterista"-inspired snare drumming

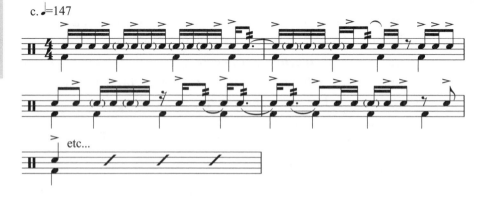

Note: This is NOT an actual transcription.

ble pedal drummers, he often uses flurries of thirty-second notes and sextuplets in his music. Usually, his double pedal flourishes add accentuation to elegant snare drum work, or they are used in combination with tom-toms and cymbals during a musical peak or climax.

Figure 14-12 combines thirty-second notes with sixteenth notes in numbers 1–4. Then, sextuplets appear in numbers 5–8. Most of these patterns move clockwise around the kit. However, numbers 7 and 8 contain cymbal flurries along with the bass drum notes. If you have two crash cymbals setup on either side of you, use those to play these patterns. If you only have a ride and one crash, use those cymbals instead. You may lead off with either hand, but obviously, you must alternate when playing these licks.

In addition to the double kick drummers discussed in Chapter 13, key double bass drummers include Carmine Appice, Rod Morgenstein, Virgil Donati, Billy Cobham, and Mike Portnoy. Then, there are drummers who use multiple bass drums, most notably Terry Bozzio and Alex Van Halen. Two bass drum set ups started in the late 1930s with the big band drummer Louie Bellson. Believe it or not, Bellson was only fifteen when he invented this set up!

Neil Peart's use of a double pedal is never gratuitous or excessive, and this is what makes his bass drumming stand out. For Peart, this technique is used simply to add another layer of sound and texture to the music. Beyond this, he is careful not to overuse his double pedals. He also doesn't use double pedal technique to cover up poor single bass drumming. Unfortunately, this is not the case with all drummers, even famous players! Overall, any serious student of rock drumming should study Peart's thoughtful and compositional approach to music for the reasons laid out in this chapter and for the simple pleasure of listening to him play. While there are "better" drummers in history—most notably Buddy Rich—there is much wisdom in Peart's methods and a lot of great drumming may be mined from his discography.

FIGURE 14-12: Technique builders for double bass drum

Track 59

Sixteenth and Thirty-second Notes

1.

2.

3.

4.

Sextuplets

5.

6.

7.

8.

Pattern #'s 1, 5, and 8 are played on the CD.

Chapter 15

Progressive Rock

In Chapter 1, you learned about the history of progressive rock. Now it's time to explore some of the most important practitioners of this broad genre. First, you will be introduced formally to Bill Bruford, one of rock's most refined and elegant drummers. Next, you will learn about Carl Palmer, who played in two of prog-rock's most popular bands: Emerson, Lake & Palmer (ELP) and Asia. And you will read about Phil Collins, who is much more than just a pop singer. At the end of the chapter, you also explore the odd time-signatures in five and seven.

Bill Bruford

Bill Bruford (born 1949) is one of the most important drummers in both rock and jazz. In fact, Bruford is one of the most creative drum set players of his generation. Blessed with a quirky but captivating approach, Bruford remains an influential voice on the drums. Additonally, Bruford is an excellent jazz-fusion composer, proving that drummers can do more than just "bash away" at the kit.

Bruford began playing the drums at the age of thirteen and was initially mesmerized by American jazz drummers Joe Morello, Max Roach, and Art Blakey. Despite his interest in jazz, by 1968, Bruford found himself involved with the art-rock or prog-rock scene in England. His breakthrough came with the band Yes. A quartet of young, talented musicians, their eponymous release, *Yes* (1969), would set the wheels in motion for a thriving career as a drummer.

With Yes, Bruford played drums on such classics as "Time and a Word," "I've Seen All Good People," "Roundabout," and "And You and I" before leaving the group to pursue other musical avenues. Soon, he joined King Crimson, an art-rock group spearheaded by guitarist Robert Fripp. Of the three albums Crimson made during this period, *Red* (1974) would become the most historically significant.

Electronic Drums Pioneer

After a brief stint as a backing drummer for Genesis, Bruford made his mark as an electronic drums innovator. In fact, he was one of the most visible endorsers of Simmons pads in the 1980s. He explored this technology with incredible success when King Crimson reformed in the early 1980s for three extraordinary albums *Discipline, Beat,* and *Three of a Perfect Pair.* Then in 1986, he formed the jazz-fusion ensemble *Earthworks* with jazz virtuosos Django Bates and Iain Ballamy. With this group, Bruford developed his highly melodic style of electronic drum set playing, and Earthworks left an indelible mark on contemporary jazz.

However, by the late 1990s, Simmons had closed shop and Bruford traded in his electronic kit for an all-acoustic setup (positioned in a symmetrical semicircle). Still, Bruford's playing never gets staid or predictable. He always remains on the cutting edge, no matter what his setup and no matter what style of music he's playing.

A Singular Voice

Throughout Bruford's career, one aspect that has never changed is his distinct snare drum ring. This ring is created by the drumhead's overtones and by the obvious lack of muffling. These overtones are further enhanced by Bruford's penchant for rim shots, hitting the rim and the head simultaneously. Indeed, this snare sound has become one of Bruford's trademarks.

Whether it's progressive rock, art rock, or jazz, Bruford has always had an affinity for complex patterns that require a great deal of limb independence. Often, he layers ostinato upon ostinato, creating a colorful rhythmical latticework. When these patterns create an x-against-x pattern, they are referred to as polyrhythms (see Chapter 2). Bruford also experiments with odd time-signatures and over-the-bar-line phrasings.

Playing Over the Bar

When you play over the bar line, you create a phrase that temporarily avoids natural resolution points. In other words, over-the-bar playing suspends the usual pauses in the music. Instead, the listener is pulled toward a superimposed time signature for an unspecified period of time. To create an over-the-bar-line pattern, drummers will intentionally play a rhythm that does not sit evenly (or easily) in the given meter. For example, the drummer might plug a 3/4 pattern inside a 4/4 time signature.

Over-the-bar-line phrasing gives music a floating or unresolved feel. It also adds tension to the music. But where there is tension, there is release. (The release is the resolution of the phrase.) It is this tension and release that makes over-the-bar-line playing so exciting. Figure 15-1 shows you one simple example of this.

FIGURE 15-1:
Over-the-bar-line tension and release

The brackets outline a repeating *three* beat phrase!

Playing in the Style of Bill Bruford

This chapter will focus on some of Bruford's most accessible beats. In prog-rock, drummers typically change grooves and feel often. It's simply the nature of the music. As mentioned in Chapter 14, prog-rock compositions also tend to fluctuate often and contain many parts. (They can be like miniature rock symphonies.) Therefore, all of the following grooves are either conglomerate patterns or underlying rhythmical skeletons intended to give you the basic flavor of the drum part. They are not actual note-for-note transcriptions.

Figure 15-2 shows one impressive groove template from the song "I've Seen All Good People," from the CD *The Yes Album*. It's one of Bruford's funkier ideas. This deep-pocketed groove is a rock shuffle. The shuffle comes from the use of triplets. The beat shown in Figure 15-2 is rather generic, but drummers playing shuffle feels have always gotten a lot of mileage out of this type of groove.

FIGURE 15-2:
"I've Seen All Good People" idea

Note: This is NOT an actual transcription.

Figure 15-3 shows how to approach the introduction and reintroduction of "Long Distance Runaround," from the album *Fragile* by Yes. In other words, this figure outlines some of the rhythmical options you could use on these sections of the tune. The reintroduction happens four times in the song and it always begins with a cymbal crash on the "and" of four. Notice how each pattern is slightly altered. However, the overall character of the groove is maintained in each of the four versions.

FIGURE 15-3:

"Long Distance Runaround" groove ideas

These variations could be played over the introduction and re-introductions.

Note: This is NOT an actual transcription.

For in-depth transcriptions of Bruford's work, check out the drummer's own publication, *When in Doubt, Roll* (see Appendix A). In this book, Bruford notates some of his most famous recorded performances, including "Heart of the Sunrise," "Beelzebub," "Frame by Frame," and others. He also includes introductory exercises designed to help you play each song.

The next pattern is from one of Yes's most famous songs, "Roundabout," which is the opening track on *Fragile*. As you might imagine, Bruford alters this pattern throughout the song. However, Figure 15-4 shows you the basic rhythmical motif that underlies his performance.

FIGURE 15-4:
"Roundabout"
basic idea

c. ♩=130

Note: This is NOT an actual transcription.

Figure 15-5 shows you a conglomerate, or mixture, of the grooves Bruford uses on the body of the song "One More Red Nightmare" from King Crimson's *Red*. This beat idea, or motif, has been chosen because it's something of a Bruford cliché. In other words, he tends to use this idea on other songs/projects as well. Among the other elements, notice the use of eighth notes in the hi-hat foot.

FIGURE 15-5:
"One More Red
Nightmare"
conglomerate
groove

c. ♩=109

Bruford also plays a fantastic rock groove on "Nerve," from the album *All Heaven Broke Loose* by Earthworks. This pattern shifts and changes, and even includes sudden meter changes. However, a basic conglomerate pattern of the main idea is indicated in Figure 15-6.

On all of the Bruford patterns notated in this chapter, be sure to use a rim shot in the snare drum. This will help you to get that "ringy" Bruford sound. Without the rim shot, your beats will lack the overtones that make Bruford's beats so instantly recognizable.

FIGURE 15-6:
"Nerve"
conglomerate
groove

c. ♩=123

Carl Palmer

Carl Palmer (born 1950) is best known for his work with the progressive-rock super group, Emerson, Lake & Palmer, and later with the prog/pop band Asia. Both groups had major successes selling millions of albums worldwide and catapulting Palmer to near legendary status. As a drummer, Palmer is known for his big band-influenced style. A "trad" grip player, Palmer grew up listening to swing-era drummers like Gene Krupa and Buddy Rich. Later he even became close friends with the inimitable Rich.

As a teen, Palmer played with his father's dance band, but eventually it was the emerging psychedelic rock movement of the late '60s that captured his interest. Soon, Palmer found himself on tour with The Crazy World of Arthur Brown, who was every bit as crazy as his band's name. Fascinated by fire, Brown performed over-the-top stage theatrics at every show. This included actually lighting himself on fire during concerts.

After leaving Brown, Palmer auditioned for a new group spearheaded by guitarist and singer Greg Lake, from King Crimson, and the virtuosic keyboardist Keith Emerson, from The Nice. As Emerson, Lake & Palmer, or ELP, Palmer's drumming was immortalized on the classic albums *Tarkus*, *Trilogy*, *Brain Salad Surgery*, and others. One of the most popular songs by this band, "Karn Evil 9," is an epic piece whose second part (once the vinyl record was flipped over) begins with the famous lyric: "Welcome back my friends to the show that never ends." On this tune, Palmer plays a famous drum break using sixteenth notes around the kit. This brief solo is an exciting flurry of snare drum and tom-tom licks together with a pounding eighth-note bass drum ostinato.

FACT

One of Carl Palmer's drum kits was made of stainless steel and weighed in at an unbelievable two-and-a-half tons. It's currently displayed at the Rock 'n' roll Hall of Fame in Cleveland, Ohio. Interestingly, The Beatles' drummer, Ringo Starr, purchased the kit and donated it to the museum.

Overall, Palmer is known for highly technical, flashy drum solos that borrow largely from Buddy Rich and other swing-era showman. This includes lightning-fast rudimental snare drum chops and intricate cross stickings. Not to be confused with a rim cross stick, cross sticking is a technique whereby the drummer crosses one hand over or under the other hand, creating an "x" shape between the arms. Cross stickings have some practical value, but they are generally used as a visual effect.

Palmer is also identified by his setup, which features double bass drums, and often, two gigantic gongs. Additionally, he's been known to use timpani and tubular bells in concert. Other career highlights include strong drum performances on the early Asia hits "Only Time Will Tell" and "Heat of the Moment" from 1982.

Phil Collins

Phil Collins (born 1951) is probably best known as a pop singer and songwriter. However, he's also an extraordinarily talented drummer. Born and raised in London, England, Collins began playing drums as a young boy. By age eighteen, he had joined a band called Flaming Youth and made an album entitled *Ark II.* However, his first big break came when he joined Genesis. Fronted by the charismatic Peter Gabriel, Collins's articulate drumming was a highlight of prog-rock classics *Nursery Cryme, Foxtrot, Selling England By the Pound,* and *The Lamb Lies Down on Broadway.* After Gabriel left Genesis to pursue a solo career, Collins fell into the role of singer. On tour, this meant hiring another drummer so Collins could sing out in front.

ESSENTIAL

With the exception of a tour featuring Bill Bruford in 1976, Genesis has worked with American session drummer Chester Thompson on virtually every tour in the post-Gabriel era. Typically, Thompson will play the bulk of the show while Collins fulfills his duties as singer and front man. Collins does, however, join Thompson behind the kit for select tunes.

Collins's most famous drum lick is a solo tom-tom fill from his song "In the Air Tonight." This song appears on the album *Face Value* (1981). A variation on this lick is shown to you in Figure 15-7. It's been changed to fit the standard three tom-tom setup used in this book. Collins, however, plays it on five tom-toms for his recording.

FIGURE 15-7:
"In the Air Tonight" tom-tom variation

c. ♩=98

Collins uses five tom-toms on this lick.
It has been reworked for three drums.

Note: This is NOT an actual transcription.

A Versatile Drummer

Collins is a versatile and technically proficient drummer whose best work is documented on early Genesis albums. Additionally, Collins displays his wares on *Unorthodox Behaviour* and *Moroccan Roll* by the fusion jazz outfit Brand X. Further, his thoughtful drumming on "No One is to Blame," by Howard Jones, shows Collins's abilities as a skillful session musician.

In 1996, Collins surprised fans by touring with his own jazz orchestra. On this tour, he did little singing; instead, his orchestra featured the voice of the legendary Tony Bennett, while Collins backed him up on drums. Collins also proved his competence as a big band drummer when he performed with The Buddy Rich Big Band in 1998 for a gala salute to the late, great drumming legend. A year later, in 1999, he also released a successful big band album entitled *A Hot Night in Paris*.

Fans of Collins also usually cite his transatlantic flight for the Live Aid Music Festival in 1985. Because of the shift in time zones, Collins was able to perform his solo material at Wembley Stadium in London then fly on the Concorde to the United States to perform with Led Zeppelin in Philadelphia, all in one day! Anyone who plays with Led Zeppelin has heavy shoes to fill.

For Collins, his performance with Zeppelin reminded listeners that he was much more than a pop star; he was a drummer to be reckoned with.

Dance on a Volcano

Figures 15-8 shows you two related grooves from Collins's progressive rock days. Both are culled from "Dance on a Volcano," the opening track on *A Trick of the Tail.* This is the first Genesis album to feature Collins as a vocalist and drummer. "Volcano" contains a tricky odd time-signature section.

Two of Collins's variations from this song are simulated in Figure 15-8. These beats are in 7/4. This means that there are seven beats in a measure and the quarter note equals one beat; it could also be written as 4/4 + 3/4. Be sure to observe the intricate open/closed hi-hats. The open hi-hat on the "and" of six is a short, sharp accent. Collins grooves over the basic, skeletal ideas shown in Figure 15-8.

FIGURE 15-8:
"Dance on a Volcano" basic ideas

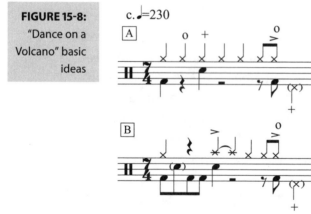

Note: This is NOT an actual transcription.

More Odd Time-Signatures

You first studied odd time-signatures in Chapter 14, but there's still much more to explore. Odd meters are common in prog-rock and other forms of art rock. They are also used occasionally in mainstream pop. Key pop examples include "Salisbury Hill" by Peter Gabriel, "Heart of Glass" by

Blondie, which features an instrumental interlude in 7/4, and "Dreaming in Metaphors" by Seal. Sting has also used odd time-signatures in his solo material (see Vinnie Colaiuta in Chapter 17).

Odd time-signatures can be a breath of fresh air if you've been listening to (or playing) lots of repetitive 4/4 grooves. However, they can also be obnoxious if they are used solely to make a song sound complex, different, and just plain weird. This book assumes that 2/2, 2/4, 3/4, 6/8, and 12/8 are relatively common-time signatures. Therefore, this chapter will focus on the time signatures 5/4, 5/8, 7/4, and 7/8. Other odd time-signatures certainly exist, and mixed meters are possible, too (as you saw in Chapter 14).

How convoluted can odd time-signatures get? The sky's the limit! You could write a song in 28/16 if you wish. However, it probably wouldn't have much musical value. Ultimately, if you're writing music or devising a drum part and you feel a groove in an odd time-signature, you should follow your instincts, throw caution to the wind, and try it out.

ALERT!

If you create songs in odd time-signatures just for the sake of doing it, you will probably leave the listener cold. Forced odd time-signatures usually sound stiff and uninviting. Odd time-signatures are tough, especially for intermediates or semi-pros, so use them only when the composition truly warrants their use.

Figure 15-9 shows you some groove possibilities in 5/4 and 5/8. In 5/4, there are five beats in a measure and the quarter note receives one beat. In 5/8, there are five beats in a measure and the eighth note receives one beat. With each beat, an attempt has been made to maintain a backbeat; this is a natural musical inclination that should be trusted.

Figure 15-10 shows you rock beats in 7/4 and 7/8. Remember, in 7/4, there are seven beats in a measure and the quarter note receives one beat. In 7/8, there are seven beats in a measure and the eighth note receives one beat. This isn't rocket science, but you'd be well advised to count carefully when you play in any odd meter. It's easy to get off, turn the beat around, or unintentionally fall back into 4/4.

FIGURE 15-9: Rock beats in 5

Track 60

In 5/4: Pattern #'s 1 and 7 are played on the CD.

in 5/8: Pattern #'s 1 and 8 are played on the CD.

FIGURE 15-10: Rock beats in 7

Beats in 7/4:

Track 61

Beats in 7/8:

In 7/4: Pattern #'s 1 and 8 are played on the CD.

in 7/8: Pattern #'s 1 and 8 are played on the CD.

Use What You Know

As you move toward the end of this book, you should take a moment to review all that you've learned. After all, you've come a long way! Since this portion of the book focuses on odd meters, think about how you might apply the skills you've learned in previous chapters to this topic.

Don't know where to start? The beats notated in figures 15-9 and 15-10 are just the tip of the iceberg when it comes to playing in odd meters. Try your own grooves in five or seven, and don't be afraid to implement the following musical devices:

- Eighth-note triplets
- Sextuplets
- Thirty-second notes (single- and double-stroke rolls)
- Buzz strokes and buzz rolls
- Accents and ghost notes
- Half-open hi-hat
- Riding on the cymbal (Don't ride on the hi-hat out of habit.)
- Using the bell of the cymbal
- Various ride ostinatos (quarter notes, sixteenth notes, rhythmic combinations)
- Two-handed riding (integrated patterns between the ride cymbal and hi-hat)
- Adding an ostinato in the hi-hat foot
- Double pedal or double bass drum

Of course, not all of these devices will work with every beat or every time signature. However, when devising beats, you should consider all the tricks you've learned in the course of your study. Then, find creative ways to implement them where possible. Remember not to overplay and to always serve the song.

Chapter 16

Stewart Copeland and Rock Hybrids

Like Chapter 14, this chapter focuses primarily on one drummer. In this case, it is Stewart Copeland, the drummer from The Police. Along with U2, The Police dominated rock and pop music in the early 1980s. However, their legacy extends far beyond this decade. This is due, in part, to Copeland's highly creative drumming style. In fact, Copeland has captured the interest of younger drummers for over twenty-five years. It's doubtful his influence will decline anytime soon.

Stewart Copeland

Along with Ringo Starr, John Bonham, and Neil Peart, Stewart Copeland (born 1952) remains one of the most significant drummers in rock. In fact, he is widely acknowledged as a brilliant innovator. Compared to the above-mentioned drummers, Copeland's style is eccentric and unconventional, but it is also probably the most identifiable. All it takes is one crack on the snare drum, one syncopated hi-hat lick, or one flourish across splash cymbals and you know who the drummer is.

Copeland is an American-born drummer from Alexandria, Virginia. The son of a CIA agent, he was raised primarily in the Middle East (Beirut, Lebanon). Many elements define Copeland's drumming style, one of which is his tendency to play on top of the beat. He's even been criticized for rushing, a charge that Copeland agrees with! He likely plays on top of the beat because his style was formed during the late 1970s, at the height of the underground punk scene in England.

FACT

In addition to his drumming, Stewart Copeland is also a noted songwriter and composer. He has scored music for movies such as *Rumble Fish, Highlander 2, Taking Care of Business, Talk Radio, Wall Street,* and others. He has also composed music for television shows such as *The Equalizer* and *Dead Like Me,* and he even wrote an opera called *Holy Blood and Crescent Moon.*

In 1978, The Police quickly embraced punk, even though Sting, a former schoolteacher, called punk "banal" on stage. If you've ever listened to punk, you can attest to its edginess. Punk never gets mellow or "chilled out." (It's the opposite of hippie rock.) It also never seeks the deep pocket like P-Funk or shuffle blues. Instead, drummers play with a lot of drive, vigor, and even reckless abandon. Depending on the band, tempos even rush, and in this context, this is not seen as bad or wrong. Like other punk-influenced drummers, Copeland's grooves are pointed and hard driving.

He plays jerky, syncopated beats. Yet somehow, they float along with great ease. Check out songs like "Next to You" from *Outlandos d'Amour,* "Driven to Tears" from *Zenyattà Mondatta,* or "Synchronicity I" from *Synchronicity.* These songs have tremendous energy and forward momentum.

If Copeland were to suddenly play with a behind-the-beat feel, like Charlie Watts for example, his style would be less effective and a lot less exciting. His tendency to nudge the tempo—though he does this less on studio releases—is actually one of his finest attributes. It wouldn't work in The Rolling Stones, for example, but it supercharges The Police's music.

Another identifiable aspect of Copeland's playing is his sound, particularly the tone he gets on his snare drum. When he plays the snare, he strikes both the head and the rim at the same time. This creates a loud "crack." Consequently, his snare drum sounds like the snap of a whip. Part of this is also due to tuning; Copeland generally tensions his snare and tom-toms tightly. This makes his tone crisp and vibrant. This tuning approach probably stems from Copeland's interest in reggae music.

QUESTIONS

What is reggae?
Reggae is a style of Latin music from Jamaica. On the drums, reggae is often marked by a cross stick/bass drum backbeat with an emphasis in the bass drum on beat three. Reggae drummers often use sudden rim shots on the snare and complex ornamentation on the hi-hat. Reggae strongly influenced Stewart Copeland's approach to rock.

Typically, reggae players use taut snare drums so they can simulate the attack of a timbale drum. Copeland's interest in reggae is both deep rooted and transparent. The Police regularly used reggae grooves in their music. For Copeland, this meant using cross-stick techniques, fancy hi-hat decorations, and unexpected cymbal crashes on upbeats. He also synthesized other ethnic music traditions into his playing. For example, Arabic music had a big impact on Copeland when he was growing up in Beirut.

Playing in the Style of Stewart Copeland

You should familiarize yourself with Copeland grooves from The Police's catalog. This groundbreaking group made five studio albums over the period of seven years (1977–1984). It's very difficult to cull basic beats from Police songs, as Copeland's style is often freewheeling. He's endlessly adding subtle variations, texture changes, and hi-hat decorations to each of his grooves. His hi-hat variations are particularly spontaneous. Because of this, no two bars are ever really the same. In spite of this, an attempt has been made to highlight some of Copeland's finest groove templates, if you will. The following figures, therefore, are not note-for-note transcriptions. Rather, they represent the skeletal ideas that inform this drummer's rather intricate style.

This first song, "Walking on the Moon," from *Reggatta de Blanc,* is a reggae-inspired pop tune. Notice the use of triplets in this beat. Copeland's groove also has a kind of swing feel to it, which is common in reggae. See Figure 16-1 for an outline of his verse and bridge patterns.

FIGURE 16-1:
"Walking on the Moon" verse and bridge ideas

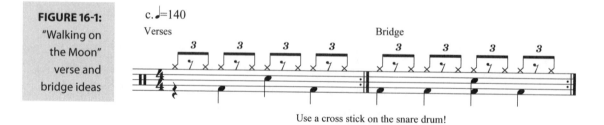

Use a cross stick on the snare drum!

Note: This is NOT an actual transcription.

"Spirits in the Material World" from *Ghost in the Machine* is another example of Copeland's Caribbean influence. This brisk ska groove uses off-beats, or "ands," in the hi-hat and a bass drum pattern on the downbeats of two and four. For the choruses, Copeland switches to a straight up rock feel with an alternating kick-snare-kick-snare backbeat. Figure 16-2 shows you a groove similar to Copeland's playing on the verses.

"Tea in the Sahara" is a reflective and beautiful Police song from *Synchronicity.* Here, Copeland plays a subtle beat employing a rhythm that could be "near triplets." In the hi-hat, he plays a triplet-like figure that has been straightened out slightly. The result is a rhythm that falls somewhere in between eighth notes and full-bore triplets. Furthermore, the sharp snare drum hit on beat four of the chorus adds just the right lift to the music. These beat ideas are illustrated in Figure 16-3.

FIGURE 16-2:
"Spirits in the Material World" verse idea

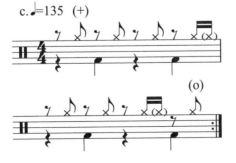

Copeland plays the notes in parenthesis ad. lib.

Note: This is NOT an actual transcription.

FIGURE 16-3:
"Tea In the Sahara" verse and chorus ideas

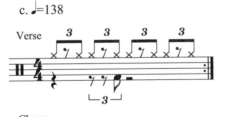

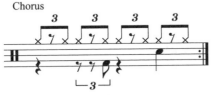

This hi-hat rhythm is *actually* played somewhere in between "straight eighths" and "triplets."

Note: This is NOT an actual transcription.

"Murder by Numbers" is another song from *Synchronicity*. Again, Copeland uses triplet-based rhythms throughout. This time, he plays twelve eighth-note triplets per bar. Additionally, on the introduction and verses, he plays every other triplet using a cross stick. For the chorus, Copeland switches to a standard two-and-four backbeat in the snare. However, the every-other-triplet concept is still maintained in the bass drum. These patterns are notated in Figure 16-4.

Figure 16-5 shows you the beat Copeland uses for the first two choruses of "Wrapped Around Your Figure," one of The Police's biggest hits. For the final chorus, the band changes the groove, giving the impression of double

FIGURE 16-4:

"Murder By Numbers" verse and chorus ideas

Use a cross stick on the verse.
Play on the snare head for the chorus.

Note: This is NOT an actual transcription.

FIGURE 16-5:

"Wrapped Around Your Finger" chorus idea

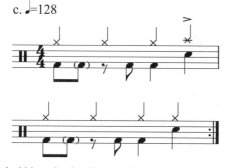

Ride on the hi-hat. On the album, a ride cymbal bell is overdubbed.

Sometimes the bass drum (and bass guitar) play the note in parenthesis; other times it's omitted.

Note: This is NOT an actual transcription.

time. Double time means to play twice the speed. In actuality, this does not occur in this tune. For the final chorus, Copeland merely plays a two-and-four backbeat opposite a bass drum pattern that was introduced earlier in the tune. However, the double-time feel creates the forward momentum needed to see the song through to its climax.

The beat you will play in Figure 16-5 includes a strong emphasis on beat four. You'll notice that the first measure of the phrase even contains a cymbal crash with the snare on beat four. This type of feel is not uncommon in popular music. In fact, it was first used on pop hits "Dead Man's Curve" (Jan and Dean), "Be My Baby" (The Ronettes), and other hits from the early to mid-1960s.

The last example, Figure 16-6, lists four Copeland clichés that you'll hear him use on a variety of songs spread across this band's discography. Look for these motifs when you hear Copeland play, especially in live settings. The first lick is used or implied by Copeland often. You'll hear him play it on the hi-hat, rack toms, or octobans. The latter are high-pitched cylindrical drums made by Tama.

FIGURE 16-6: Copeland clichés

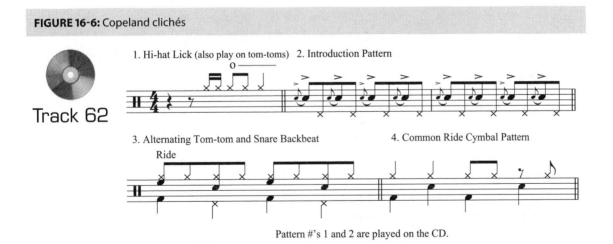

Pattern #'s 1 and 2 are played on the CD.

Advanced Hi-Hat Techniques

The remainder of this chapter focuses on beats and fills inspired by Copeland. As previously mentioned, Copeland is known for his elaborate hi-hat work. Sometimes Copeland used studio echo to create these hi-hat embellishments. For example, he does this on "Walking on the Moon." However, in a live context he found himself recreating the effect of the echo, leading to complex embellishments.

FACT

Without a doubt, fancy hi-hat work has become one of Copeland's signatures. Peter Gabriel even featured Copeland on solo hi-hat for the opening of his song "Red Rain," from the album *So*. In actuality, Copeland's hi-hat work is impossible to notate with specificity. This is because it contains too many different colors and shades.

As you know, in standard notation, hi-hat sounds are written using open symbols, half-open symbols, and closed symbols. But Copeland uses more refined gradients of open and closed. For example, you might hear a note that exists somewhere in between half open and closed. Unless you create your own system, there are no musical symbols for this. Despite the limitations of notation, Figure 16-7 shows you some hi-hat ornamentations that you can use as a point of departure.

What's nice about hi-hat embellishments is that they generally sound subtle to the listener. Therefore, you can use them on just about any pop song without losing the groove of overplaying. Only open (o) and closed (+) hi-hat symbols have been used in Figure 16-7. However, you should experiment with other gradients, too. To create other sounds, use varying amounts of pressure as you push down on the pedal.

In Figure 16-7 you will notice the use of a five-stroke roll in pattern number 2, a three-stroke ruff in pattern number 5, and a four-stroke ruff in pattern number 6. These patterns are written with a repeat for practicing purposes. However, Copeland rarely uses repeating ostinatos when it comes to hi-hat embellishments. Therefore, feel free to use these patterns in conjunction with other beats and fills. For example, you might want to use them as a quick changeup or as a beat-fill combination. If you've forgotten what the latter is, see Chapter 9.

FIGURE 16-7: Fancy hi-hat embellishments

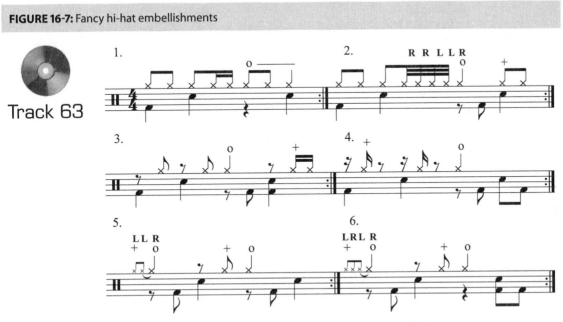

Track 63

Pattern #'s 1 and 5 are played on the CD.

Sixteenth-Note Bursts and Quarter-Note Triplets

Copeland is also very fond of using what could be termed "sixteenth-note bursts." Typically, Copeland will throw in two sixteenth notes to add an unexpected burst of color. He usually does not use these licks like a traditional fill. In other words, he doesn't use them to indicate the end/beginning of a phrase or the end/beginning of a song section. Instead, he uses sixteenth-note bursts to add unanticipated variation to his beats. In Figure 16-8, you will see a four-bar reggae groove with sixteenth-note bursts added in. Always play these bursts using single-stroke stickings so the sixteenth notes pop out of the fabric of the music.

Next, try a groove inspired by the verses of "Demolition Man" (*Ghost in the Machine*). Here this groove is paired with sixteenth-note bursts. Again, a four-bar phrase is used here. See Figure 16-9.

FIGURE 16-8: Four-bar reggae groove using sixteenth-note bursts

Track 64

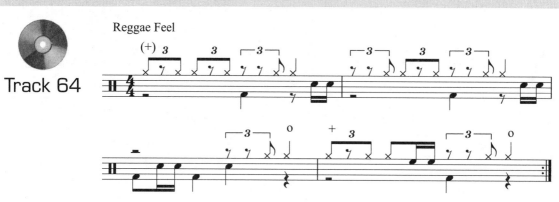

FIGURE 16-9: Sixteenth-note bursts with "Demolition Man" groove

Track 65

You may also ride on the cymbal using the tip of the stick on the bell.

Note: This is NOT an actual transcription.

Now it's time to experiment with the quarter-note triplets. This is another common rhythm Copeland uses. The quarter-note triplet is actually widespread in many styles of Latin music, especially Afro-Cuban or salsa milieus. Reggae drummers also use it frequently. Often, Copeland will use quarter-note triplets in conjunction with the aforementioned sixteenth-note bursts.

Figure 16-10 shows you the basic groove from "Hole in My Life," from *Outlandos d'Amour,* together with a Copeland-inspired quarter-note triplet lick. As you will see, the hidden quarter-note triplets are spread across beats two and three in measure two. These are written as eighth-note triplets (with rests) because it's easier to read over-the-beat triplets this way. When writing quarter-note triplets, its best to keep beats one and two bracketed together and beats three and four bracketed together. When writing a triplet pattern that moves from beat two to beat three, you should break up the notation as you see in Figure 16-10.

In general, quarter-note triplets can be applied to anything with a swing or reggae feel. Listen for Copeland slyly inserting them when you least expect it. He uses them quite effectively in the hi-hat breakdown for "Walking on the Moon." He also spruces up the song "Driven to Tears," from *Zenyatta Mondatta,* with quarter-note triplet fills.

FIGURE 16-10:
Quarter-note triplets with "Hole in My Life" groove

Hidden quarter-note triplets

One fill option Copeland might play.

Note: This is NOT an actual transcription.

Advanced Cross Stick Rhythms

More than any other drummer in rock, Copeland is known for his use of extensive rim play. For him, the cross stick is a colorful sound that has many applications. As previously mentioned, his interest in cross sticks comes from his fascination with reggae music. However, in many ways, he took this technique to new levels. Early on, Copeland used studio echo to create dazzling cross stick rhythms. This is best evidenced on the song "Reggatta de Blanc," from the album of the same name. Here, he plays various sixteenth-note combinations using single- and double-stroke cross sticks and a closed hi-hat. Then, echo is placed overtop to increase the density of the pattern. Later uses do not feature echo, but the musical impact of his cross stick patterns are no less impressive.

Figure 16-11 shows one possible cross stick/hi-hat improvisation Copeland might play. These rhythms may also be played between the rim and the ride cymbal. You will notice that this exercise contains four-on-the-floor in the bass drum. This means that the kick drum plays repetitive downbeats on 1, 2, 3, and 4. The hi-hat mostly plays eighth notes in the first four bars, but as you enter into the last phrase, it switches to a highly interactive sixteenth-note pattern between the hands. This pattern, by the way, is based on the rhythms Copeland plays on the song "Reggatta de Blanc."

FIGURE 16-11: Using a cross stick

Track 66

In this exercise, don't forget to use a *cross stick* on the snare!

ALERT!

As always, start slowly at first. Reading and playing the music accurately is more important than speed. Also, make sure you get a good cross stick sound. As mentioned in Chapter 12, it's important to find the sweet spot when playing cross sticks. If you don't, your patterns will sound thin and delicate and they will not be heard amidst the roar of guitars, keyboards, bass, etc.

Splashes and Bells

Copeland was one of the first to use splash cymbals individualistically. The big band drummers of old used them as an occasional effect, and before them, traditional jazz drummers used small "zinger" cymbals mounted on their bass drums. However, Copeland integrated splash cymbals into his fills quite resourcefully. Later, drummers such as Manu Katche, Carter Beauford, and Vinnie Colaiuta would also use splashes very creatively.

The splash is a small cymbal ranging 6"–12". The best sizes for splashes are 6" and 8". For the 2007–2008 Police Reunion tour, Copeland's setup featured two splashes and another tiny, thick cymbal known as a signature bell. His classic setup contained three splashes and two signature bells. He's always used Paiste cymbals, but many other cymbal manufacturers also make great splashes (see Appendix B).

Signature bells are not commonly used by drum set players. However, they are available through Paiste if you want to experiment with them or if you want to recreate Copeland's sound more authentically. However, splashes should suffice. These cymbals are readily available in stores (various manufacturers) and they are a fun to use.

The sound splashes and bells make are very different. Splashes are ultra-thin cymbals that offer a quick, short "splash" sound. They sound similar to a glass cup or a light bulb when they fall and break. As you might imagine, this is an attention-grabbing sound. However, the decay is fast; splashes do not ring out for more than a second or two. Bells, on the other hand, have a chime effect since they are heavy cymbals. When you strike a bell, the sound is high pitched. It also resonates longer and the decay is slower than a splash. Since bells are less common, this book will focus on the splash cymbal. Figure 16-12 shows you a four-bar exercise complete with syncopated splashes. To keep things simple, only one splash is employed here. However, if you have a couple in your setup, feel free to implement both of them as you wish.

Splashes are generally used as an accent cymbal. They can be used like regular-sized crashes to signify song transitions, like the end of a phrase or the beginning of a song section. However, as you will see in Figure 16-12, the splash is normally used to add color, texture, and depth to beats. You may also use them in the middle of a fill like a tom-tom.

Unlike regular-sized crash cymbals, splashes may be played solo or by themselves. You do not necessarily need bass drum or snare drum accompaniment. However, if you do use a splash like a traditional crash cymbal, you will want to add a bass drum or snare drum note underneath the splash. Above all else, have fun with splashes—as Copeland does. They can be an effective addition to your setup, as long as you use them tastefully.

FIGURE 16-12: Using a splash cymbal

Track 67

All crashes used in this example should be played on a splash cymbal!

Chapter 17

Jazz-Rock and a New Breed of Drummers

This is the last chapter to focus on specific drummers. Here, you will learn about fusion or jazz-rock. You will also be formally introduced to some of the finest drummers in the world; players such as Tony Williams, Billy Cobham, Vinnie Colaiuta, Dave Weckl, and Steve Gadd are in the top echelon of drumming. Last, but not least, you will learn about female drummers and their many contributions. Long overlooked, women drummers are now getting the respect they are due.

Defining Fusion

Broadly speaking, any style of music could be called fusion. How can this be? You'd be hard pressed to find a style of music that doesn't draw from other sources. All musical styles have precursors. A genre is really the result of other musical genres fusing together in some unique way. Therefore, all music is "fusion."

Despite this, when people say fusion in a musical context, they're referring to a combination of jazz and rock also called jazz-rock. Fusion was first developed in the late 1960s. As a genre, its heyday was the 1970s. However, when the New Orleans "young lions" emerged in the 1980s—spearheaded by the Marsalis brothers—jazz's preoccupation with fusion diminished.

At this time, bebop and even more traditional forms of jazz took center stage, while fusion, as a category, dipped in popularity. Despite this, fusion has enjoyed several resurgences and comebacks, especially since its definition has been expanded to include funk-jazz, reggae-jazz, rap-jazz, and even metal-jazz. Combining jazz with other styles is just too enticing!

Classic Fusion

Classic 1970s fusion is marked by the use of acoustic and electric instruments such as electric guitars and early synthesizers. It rarely features vocals and the music tends to be virtuosic in nature. Fusion songs also tend to be quite involved. Like prog-rock, fusion has been criticized for being long-winded. For example, Miles Davis's "Bitches Brew" is twenty-seven minutes long. However, fans of the genre enjoy fusion for its complexity and length.

FACT

Fusion began percolating in the late 1960s. Early jazz-rock releases *In a Silent Way* and *Bitches Brew* by Miles Davis were hugely influential, as was Tony Williams's *Emergency!* By the mid 0s, fusion was a mainstay and groups such as Mahavishnu Orchestra, Weather Report, and Return to Forever dominated the scene.

Fans and Artists

Despite the changes that have occurred over the decades, fusion is generally music for musicians and wannabe musicians. Its use of odd meters and technical expertise make this music especially popular among lesser musicians—typically amateur, semi-pro, and journeyman musicians—who are wowed by the skill level of fusion artists. Dedicated practitioners are very often rhythm-section musicians: guitarists, bassists, and drummers. On guitar, John McLaughlin, Pat Metheny, Mike Stern, Allan Holdsworth, and Al Di Meola are top dogs. It's important to note that their individual styles vary greatly, though.

Key bassists include Stanley Clarke, Jeff Berlin, Mark Egan, Anthony Jackson, John Patitucci, and the incomparable Jaco Pastorius. Then there are the bands. Groups such as Vital Information, Steps Ahead, Tribal Tech, Fourplay, and Spyro Gyra remain popular. Some of these groups also helped usher in a subgenre of fusion called smooth jazz, which appeals to a wider fan base. Steely Dan is another genre-bending group that must be mentioned here. One of the most creative bands in modern history, Steely Dan combines jazz, funk, R&B, and pop into a beautiful musical tapestry. If you haven't heard them yet, do yourself a favor and check this group out.

Drummers and Fusion

Fusion is particularly welcoming to drummers, who get to play with all the force and drive that comes natural to the instrument. However, unlike straight-up pop and rock, fusion drummers are also free to play the complex technical gymnastics drummers crave. All this makes fusion drumming rather desirable—if you're good enough to cut the mustard! You are expected to have monster chops to play this music.

Drummers Lenny White, Chad Wackerman, Dennis Chambers, Gary Husband, Danny Gottlieb, Gregg Bissonette, Steve Smith, Joel Rosenblatt, Omar Hakim, Terry Bozzio, and Joey Baron are among the finest modern drummers. It's no doubt they have all gravitated toward fusion music.

Tony Williams

Tony Williams (1945–1997) is known for his abilities as a contemporary jazz drummer. He appeared on the scene at the ripe age of thirteen, performing with Sam Rivers, and later, Jackie McLean. By seventeen, Williams was invited to join Miles Davis Quintet. He played in this legendary quintet for six years, appearing on well over a dozen albums with Davis. After he left Davis, Williams started his own fusion project, Lifetime, with organist Larry Young, guitarist John McLaughlin, and later, Cream bass player Jack Bruce. However, Williams never strayed too far from his associations with former Miles Davis band mates Wayne Shorter, Herbie Hancock, and Ron Carter. In fact, he performed on and off with them for the rest of his life.

Williams is known for his fluid style, derived, in part, from his teacher Alan Dawson, a respected jazz drummer from the Boston area. Williams also was an explosive drummer, not unlike Elvin Jones. According to a 1996 interview for BET Jazz, he claimed that successful musicians are not afraid to fail. This philosophy permeated his playing, which was fearless at every turn. His approach was heavy hitting but sensitive, over the top but musical; he really had all the bases covered. He could swing like Art Blakey, rock as hard as John Bonham, and solo like the showmen of the swing era. However, unlike classic big band drummers, Williams could stun you with unconventional melodic ideas and knotty polymetrics (playing in two different time signatures at once).

As a jazz-rock player, Williams is known for his washy cymbal grooves and funky, hard-driving backbeats. Unfortunately, Williams died unexpectedly at age fifty-one after a routine gall bladder surgery. Figure 17-1 shows you a groove simulation he plays on the song "Mr. Spock." You can hear the exact beat and variations on the album *Lifetime: A Collection*. Notice the use

FIGURE 17-1:
"Mr. Spock"
groove idea

Tony Williams varies this beat ad lib.

of the eighth-two sixteenth ride ostinato, which was first introduced in Figure 11-4. Williams uses this universal ostinato and adds an open hi-hat on the downbeats.

Another memorable groove by Williams is heard on the song "Red Mask," from the compilation *The Best of Tony Williams.* Here, Williams plays a funky shuffle pattern toward the beginning of the piece. This rhythm exists somewhere in between sixteenth notes and sixteenth-note triplets. Since it's slanted more in the direction of the latter, it is shown to you in Figure 17-2 using sextuplets. Be sure to play the half-open hi-hats, and don't forget the accents.

FIGURE 17-2:
"Red Mask"
opening
groove idea

Use a half-open hi-hat (⊗) on this beat.

Note: This is NOT an actual transcription.

Billy Cobham

Billy Cobham (born 1944) is one of fusion's most revered musicians on any instrument. He was raised in New York City, where he likely first heard great jazz. After serving in the U.S. Army band, Cobham began an impressive career that would see the drummer perform with many of the leading lights in jazz and fusion. While he is best known for his drumming on the Miles Davis jazz-rock albums *A Tribute to Jack Johnson, Bitches Brew, On the Corner,* and the Mahavishnu Orchestra albums *Inner Mounting Flame* and *Birds of Fire,* Cobham has appeared literally on hundreds of albums. These range from nearly two dozen solo releases to work with pianist Horace Silver, sessions with guitarist Kenny Burrell, and even soundtrack work with pop artist Peter Gabriel.

Cobham is a deep-pocketed groove player, an explosive soloist, and fiery accompanist. He often uses sudden bursts of notes or flurries of thirty-second notes around his large drum kit. Be sure to listen to his blistering single-stroke rolls! Cobham's also a skillful double bass drummer, who uses his double kick to add intensity and depth to his sound.

Photographs of Cobham show him performing on right-handed and left-handed kits. When his kit is set up righty, he still rides lefty, placing the ride cymbal off to his left side. In the 1980s, he switched to power tom-toms (deeper drums), and his huge setup started to resemble a heavy metal drummer's kit. However, no matter how hard Cobham hits, his style is still firmly rooted in jazz.

Vinnie Colaiuta

It's silly to talk about who the best all-around drummer in the world is. However, if pressed, Vinnie Colaiuta (born 1956) could very well hold this distinction, at least among those living today. It's hard to imagine another drummer possessing greater command of the instrument. He can play funk, swing, rock, Latin, and virtually any other style with complete authority. He can play flashy or understated, full throttle or sensitive, complex and eccentric or deep-pocketed, simple, and sparse. Virtually every beat and lick this drummer plays is creative, tasty, and unwaveringly precise. If that wasn't enough, he's also reputed to be one of the finest sight-readers in the history of the instrument.

Colaiuta is from Brownsville, Pennsylvania, but is known for his prolific career as a session master in Los Angeles, California. He got his first drum set at age fourteen, and by twenty-two he scored his first major gig playing with the zany but brilliant guitarist and composer Frank Zappa. With Zappa, Colaiuta played on numerous albums, including the now classic *Tinsel Town Rebellion* and *Shut Up 'n Play Yer Guitar.* However, his most stunning performance with Zappa is *Joe's Garage.* An off-color rock opera, composed in three acts, *Joe's Garage* features Colaiuta's drumming throughout, especially on the tracks "A Token of My Extreme," "Keep in Greasey," and "He Used To Cut the Grass."

In addition to Zappa, Colaiuta has worked with Herbie Hancock, Faith Hill, Joni Mitchell, Megadeth, and scores more.

Colaiuta is also feted for his work with Sting, the ex-Police front man. Figure 17-3 shows you two patterns Colaiuta might improvise over "Seven Days" *(Ten Summoner's Tales)*. The first pattern outlines the intro and verse beats. The second pattern shows you a beat-fill combination that can be used to segue into verse one. Both examples are written in 5/4.

Figure 17-4 is another odd time-signature pattern beat inspired by "St. Augustine in Hell," from *Ten Summoner's Tales*. This is the basic groove template that Colaiuta plays over. It's written in 7/4, and because the ride pattern

FIGURE 17-3:
"Seven Days"
variations

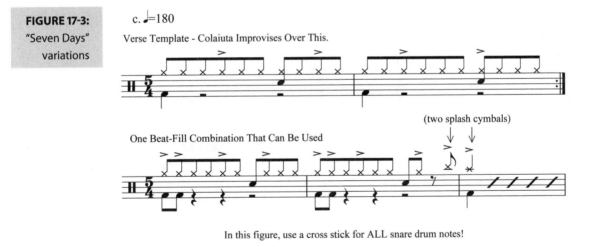

In this figure, use a cross stick for ALL snare drum notes!

Note: This is NOT an actual transcription.

FIGURE 17-4:
"St. Augustine
in Hell" basic
idea

Remember, diamond-shaped noteheads indicate cymbal bell.

Note: This is NOT an actual transcription.

is evenly spaced (half notes), it floats over the bar line, returning on beat one only after it has cycled for two measures.

Moving back in time, Colaiuta's drumming on *Joe's Garage* is simply classic. Check out his introduction to the song "Keep it Greasey." Notice the subtle variation in the groove from measure to measure. Also, if you listen to the track, notice how colorful his ride-cymbal pattern sounds as he moves back and forth between the body and bell of the ride. Figure 17-5 shows an outline of the groove, minus the added cymbal play. Think of this as a skeleton beat inspired by the introduction.

The last example, Figure 17-6, shows you the basic ostinato used on *Shut Up 'n Play Yer Guitar*. Here, Colaiuta expertly solos over this pattern using polyrhythms and over the bar-line phrasings. You should try your hand improvising over this same odd-time ostinato. Bear in mind, though, you will have to play much simpler than Colaiuta. That's okay!

FIGURE 17-5:
"Keep it Greasey" inspired improvisation

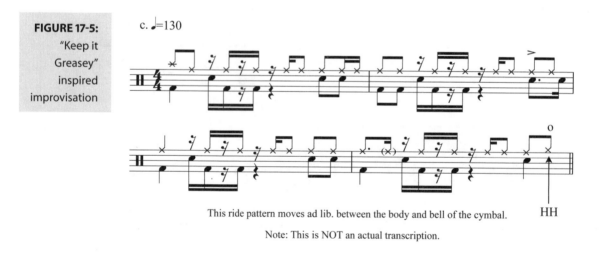

This ride pattern moves ad lib. between the body and bell of the cymbal. HH

Note: This is NOT an actual transcription.

FIGURE 17-6:
"Five-Five-Five" ostinato

Try soloing over this ostinato!

First, learn the basic ostinato. Then, break it up around the kit. After this, practice soloing over it using a variety of rhythms and phrasings. Be sure to use a metronome, and don't forget to at least imply the ostinato as you solo. It's not easy, but you can do it!

Dave Weckl

Without a doubt, Dave Weckl (born 1960) is one of the world's finest drum set players. Most quality drummers can't even dream of playing the things he does. He's a complete drumming machine. Unfortunately, Weckl's precision and perfection have garnered criticism over the years from those who want their drummers to sound more organic, earthy, and frankly, human.

Perhaps Weckl himself has reflected on these criticisms, because around 1996 he went back to the proverbial woodshed and changed his entire approach to drumming. As a student of teaching guru Freddie Gruber, Weckl began to play, as he put it, "less athletic" and more "natural." In fact, he changed his entire method, even the way he grips the sticks. Musically, Weckl's musical focus has also shifted away from flashy solos to deep-pocketed, funky grooves. This was marked by his 1998 solo release *Rhythm of the Soul*, which culled more from R&B than slick '90s fusion.

FACT

Dave Weckl was raised in St. Charles, Missouri. After college in Connecticut, he moved to New York City, where he took the Big Apple by storm. His big break came when he was asked to join Chick Corea's Elektric Band in the mid-1980s. This decision made him a favorite among *Modern Drummer* readers. As of this writing, Weckl has released nearly a dozen successful solo albums.

Despite Weckl's new approach to drumming, a quick listen still reveals complex grooves and heady solos. To some, this is showy and excessive. To others, it is mind blowing. Whatever your opinion, it's important to recognize that Weckl is a rare talent.

Figure 17-7 shows you a groove template (not a note-for-note transcription) that Weckl plays on the song "Lucky Seven" (*Synergy*). This is a rock pattern in 7/4 that uses an eighth–two sixteenth ride pattern and open hi-hats. Weckl's groove has wider applications in other 7/4 settings, so be creative and experiment.

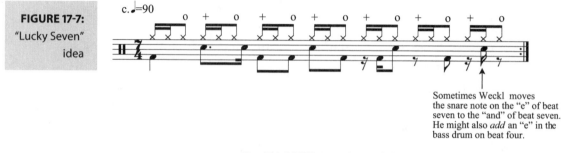

Sometimes Weckl moves
the snare note on the "e" of beat
seven to the "and" of beat seven.
He might also *add* an "e" in the
bass drum on beat four.

Note: This is NOT an actual transcription.

Steve Gadd

Steve Gadd (born 1945) is a drummer who plays a wide variety of music from straight-ahead jazz to knotty fusion to Latin montunos to pop rock. Gadd was born and raised in Rochester, New York. He first cut his teeth performing with Chuck Mangione (flugelhorn) and his bandleader brother, Gap (piano). It's hard to say where all the hot shot fusion drummers would be today if Gadd had never existed. From authentic forays to Afro-Cuban music to creative combinations of funk, jazz, and pop, Gadd's done it all.

Gadd's style has always been fluid, melodic, and elegant. He uses ghost notes to create depth and layers in his grooves, and he regularly employs linear patterns between the snare and the hi-hat or the snare and the ride cymbal. Gadd's also very rudimental based. This stems from his youth, when he played in marching bands. Without a doubt, Gadd has had a major impact on contemporary drumming and the schooled drummer can't escape his influence, like it or not. Like Tony Williams, Gadd's contribution is simply too significant.

Steve Gadd appears on some 600 albums! Highlights include stints with Paul Simon, Eric Clapton, Al DiMeola, George Benson, and Chick Corea, plus classic performances on Chet Baker's *She Was Too Good To Me* and Steely Dan's *Aja*. He's also released many albums with his own band, The Gadd Gang.

Gadd's most famous drumming is featured on the Paul Simon tunes "50 Ways to Leave Your Lover" and "Late In The Evening." On the latter, Gadd uses two pairs of sticks to simulate the sound (and density) of a Cuban percussion section. Figure 17-8 shows you an improvisation over his groove on "50 Ways to Leave Your Lover." This pattern is a sly combination of marching rhythms and swampy funk syncopations.

FIGURE 17-8:
"50 Ways to Leave Your Lover" improvisation

Sometimes Gadd plays the hi-hat foot note in parenthesis; other times he omits it.

Note: This is NOT an actual transcription.

A New Breed of Drummers

The twenty-first century is clearly the century of music education. Despite cutbacks in music programs in public schools, young people are learning more about music than ever before. This includes drum set playing. In fact, for the first time, the drum set is starting to get the respect it deserves. Over the last fifteen years, discrimination against the drum set in institutional settings has declined, and more than ever, music schools are welcoming the drum set as a legitimate instrument.

Additionally, the Internet and the publishing industry have made it possible for young drummers to study the drum set from a variety of credible sources. Concert footage can be seen with a click of a mouse (on YouTube) and specific recorded tracks can be purchased in MP3 format with ease. Most of all, dozens of superb drum set books have hit the market over the last fifteen years. For students eager to demystify the tricks of the trade, these books have proven to be invaluable.

The result is that droves of phenomenal drummers are suddenly appearing on the scene. Moreover, top drummers can do more now than most top players could have dreamed of even twenty-five years ago. Like tennis and hockey, the game has changed.

The Emergence of Women

Another change that has occurred in the drumming community is the growing number of women drummers. Historically, women have had little impact on the drum set. This is because, with very few exceptions, women didn't play the drum set. It just wasn't done. The untrained Maureen "Moe" Tucker was an early pioneer. Performing with the Velvet Underground in the 1960s, Tucker's unusual setup and arty approach to the drums was well received. However, it did little to kindle the spirit of drumming in most women, as evidenced by the paucity of female drummers to emerge in the wake of VU's demise. In the same decade, Karen Carpenter made her debut with her brother Richard in a duo simply called The Carpenters. A committed drummer, Carpenter showed her skill and dynamism on early Carpenters's recordings. However, she was gradually persuaded to sing rather than drum, and on later albums, male drummers had all but replaced her in the studio.

FACT

Over the last ten years, Sheila E. has toured on and off with Ringo Starr and His All Star Band. In past tours, she was featured in a comical drum battle with Starr himself, who played the foil to her dazzling artistry. Blending Latin rhythms with masterful hand technique, Sheila E. is recognized as one of the finest drummers of her generation.

In the 1980s, Gina Schock of The Go-Go's brought greater acceptance of women behind the kit. However, lingering sexism still relegated most women drummers to all-girl bands. It wasn't until Sheila E. was featured with Prince that women drummers were finally taken seriously by the male-dominated entertainment industry. An expert timbalero and hand drummer, Sheila E. was also a superb drum set player whose talents were regularly promoted by Prince. To this day, Sheila E. asserts her brilliance on percussion instruments, behind the kit, and in front of the microphone.

Cindy Blackman and Terri Lyne Carrington

In the 1990s, Cindy Blackman and Terri Lyne Carrington arrived on the music scene with jaw-dropping results. Mentored by Alan Dawson and Jack DeJohnette, respectively, these drummers proved, like Sheila E., that skill, limb independence, dexterity, endurance, sensitivity, and power behind the kit had nothing to do with gender.

In 1993, Blackman's breakthrough came when she was hired to play with rocker Lenny Kravitz, a gig she kept for eleven years. However, she has also played with some of the most celebrated legends of jazz and jazz-fusion. These include Jackie McLean, Joe Henderson, Don Pullen, Pharoah Sanders, Bill Laswell, and others. She has also led a successful solo career, blending together funk and jazz on nine solo albums to date. Each one boasts an all-star roster of musicians, including Wallace Roney, Kenny Barron, Ron Carter, and many other top names in music.

Terri Lyne Carrington's drumming is similarly impressive. Her virtuosic skills have landed her gigs with jazz greats Stan Getz, James Moody, Lester Bowie, David Sanborn, and many others. Combining funky elements with bebop phrasing, technical wizardry, and R&B soulfulness, Carrington has bridged the gap between jazz and rock styles much like her male counterparts Dave Weckl, Vinnie Colaiuta, and Dennis Chambers. Other fine players such as Kim Thompson (Mike Stern) and Hilary Jones (Lee Ritenour, Doc Severinsen) have followed suit with burgeoning careers of their own.

It seems certain that the new breed of drummers will likely feature many more women in the coming decades. It also seems certain that most newcomers will display a level of skill and versatility that previous generations lacked; such is the beautiful and exciting nature of progress.

Chapter 18

Concepts for Success

This chapter contains some common-sense advice about how to get gigs, build a strong reputation, and excel in this often-cutthroat industry. There are thousands of drummers out there and even thousands more wannabe drummers. Where do you fit in? It's not just about having the fastest left hand or the most thunderous double bass drum shuffle. The good drummer is more comprehensive. On the following pages, you will learn about the most important components for success.

Attitude Counts

More and more, drummers are becoming prima donnas. This is a relatively new and strange phenomenon. It is true that drummers used to be the butt of most jokes and that band leaders often referred to their band as "x musicians and a drummer." However, now that drummers are starting to get the respect they deserve, some of them are overcompensating and developing arrogant attitudes. A good drummer knows that his prime directive is to be a superlative accompanist. With the exception of a few art-rock, prog-rock, and metal substyles, rock and pop drumming generally means supporting singers and soloists. It also means locking in rhythmically with the bass player. If you do these two tasks well—supporting and locking—you are performing your primary job as a drummer. Playing fancy-schmancy solos is fun, but, alas, it is secondary. Sorry, Buddy Rich fans!

FACT

Immature drummers feel they should be the musical focus. When they are not, they cop an attitude. Some even overplay with the intention of not so subtly inserting their personality and agenda into the music. However, the good drummer takes pride in playing a supportive role; he glues the ensemble together. He doesn't peel it apart through excessive or egotistical playing.

Your musicianship is determined first by your attitude. If you let your ego control your playing, you will likely play inappropriately. Rock drummers Ringo Starr, Charlie Watts, Levon Helm, Don Henley, and others may not have exceptional chops, and they're clearly not showmen, but they get the job done right. For this, they are considered great players by many of their peers and fellow musicians.

Moreover, tasteful session drummers Hal Blaine, Steve Gadd, Andy Newmark, Jim Keltner, Russ Kunkel, Bernard Purdie, Jeff Porcaro, and John J.R. Robinson became successful and sought after because they all approached music from the standpoint of serving the song. No matter what style of music you're playing, if you live by this philosophy, you will be more successful, popular, and employable.

The Home Recording Advantage

Home recording has made remarkable changes over the last twenty-five years or so. Prior to the digital age, most home recording was done on multitrack cassette decks. Tascam's Portastudio was especially popular in the early '80s. These machines allowed people to record up to eight tracks, but the sound quality could not compete with the two-inch tape, reel-to-reel, and console setups found in professional studios.

By the mid-1980s, Digital Audio Tape (DAT) recorders became a feasible home recording option, but this was limited to recording live to two-track. In 1991, the Alesis Digital Audio Tape (ADAT) was introduced, allowing aficionados to record up to eight tracks onto Super VHS magnetic tape. Despite the promise of this technology, home-recording engineers still needed to bounce tracks down, or synchronize machines together, if they wanted to record more than eight tracks.

If you're new to home recording, try Apple's GarageBand. GarageBand is a great primer for recording enthusiasts. This software application allows you to build loops from their collection of instrument samples. Furthermore, you can record your own instruments by using an interface or a microphone. There are also fun reverbs, EQ settings, and easy editing options.

Today, home computers are used to create recordings with professional results. If you have good ears, reasonable computer skill, sufficient workspace, and a lot of patience, you can record your music at home. To get started, all you need is a Mac or PC, and a Digital Audio Workstation (DAW) such as Pro Tools, Nuendo, Cubase, Logic, Digital Performer, or Sonar. Next, you need an interface and an array of quality plug-ins (reverbs, compressors, and equalizers). If you plan on recording acoustic or live instruments, you will also need some decent microphones. Once you learn how to use this technology, you can engineer and produce your own music. The beauty of this is that you no longer have to pay expensive studio and engineering fees.

Recording to Learn

Recording at home is extremely educational. In fact, the recording process will help you improve your overall skill as a drummer. Past generations of music students had few opportunities to record their playing, and laying down tracks in a professional studio was trial by fire. But today, you can practice recording at home. Among other things, if you record yourself regularly, you can better measure your progress, and this will help you better structure your practice routine. Recording might even become part of your practice routine.

ESSENTIAL

When you record, you can evaluate your strengths and weaknesses by listening back to each take. As you listen back to each recorded performance, you will be able to assume the role of teacher. Once you remove yourself from the mechanics of performing, you can observe more objectively.

By critically reviewing your recorded performances, you will be able to hear yourself as others hear you. This is an invaluable resource, especially if you do not take private lessons. Analyzing your playing in real time is hard to do. However, if you go back and listen to what you played, you will be able to appraise your performance with more insight and clarity.

Do you need to record with a band? Not always. Recording with a band is optimal, but it is not essential. Even without a backing group, you will learn a lot by recording yourself playing alone. Despite this, try to find one or two people to sit in with you on your home recordings. Guitarists, bassists, and keyboardists are ideal. However, virtually any instrumentalist will do.

Listening Tips

When listening to recordings of your drumming, you need to ask yourself revealing questions. Below are some key questions to bear in mind:

- **Timekeeping.** Ask yourself, "Do I keep steady time?" If not, spend more time with a metronome. If you don't already know it, time-keeping is the #1 job of a drummer.
- **Rhythmical accuracy.** You might be keeping time, but are the rhythms within the time sloppy? Ask yourself, "Are my rhythms clean and articulate? Moreover, do I play with intent and confidence?" If not, again, practice with a metronome. If you're having a lot of problems with rhythm, buy a beginner snare drum method book like *Alfred's Drum Method, Book I*, and work your way through each lesson. This will help you better understand common rhythms, and hopefully, it will fill in any gaps or holes in your knowledge.
- **Sound and appropriateness.** Ask yourself, "Am I creating an attractive and expressive sound on the drums?" If not, think about how you're striking the drumheads and cymbals. Are you using proper grip and form? Also, ask yourself if your drums are in good shape. Do you have worn out, dented heads or hairline cracks in your cymbals? If so, it's time to purchase some new gear. If you're playing with other musicians, think about whether or not your drum parts complement the other musicians in the band, particularly the bass player and singer. If there is a soloist, are you playing rhythms/grooves that fit well with the solo? At the end of the day, drummers who play with taste and sensitivity are the most revered.

Furthermore, think about dynamics and the amount of notes you're playing. Are you playing too loud? Too soft? Too busy? Too spare? Are you driving the music or do you sound weak and logy? Does the music feel good or does it feel stiff and mechanical? Feel is everything in drums! Other musicians don't really care if you can play a double paradiddle at 400 beats per minute. However, they do care about how good your feel is. They like drummers who give the music proper grounding. If you do this, you're likely to get called back to play again. If you don't, you may find yourself sitting at home waiting for the phone to ring.

Playing in a Band

Playing in a band can be either a rewarding or frustrating experience. It all depends on the circumstance and, most of all, your outlook. If you approach group playing with realistic expectations, your life will be enriched. However, if you have naive goals or an overly idealistic perspective, you may find that playing in a band is frustrating or even downright maddening.

In order to pave the road for success, start by finding like-minded musicians. You will quickly find yourself alienated or even at loggerheads with your band members if you chose the wrong people. One of the best ways to find like-minded musicians is to go see local bands perform. If you don't know of any local groups, get out there and scope out the scene. Read local reviews and check out the club listings in the newspaper. These days, you might also use *www.myspace.com* or *www.facebook.com* to network, as long as you are careful to avoid the obvious spam. Furthermore, if your city has a *www.craigslist.org* page, you can often meet other musicians through musicians' classified ads.

ALERT!

If your band becomes popular, the songwriters of the group will get the lion's share of the profits. This is because most of the money comes from publishing. Therefore, it's in your best interest to either cowrite the songs or sign an interband agreement that spells out, in legal terminology, each member's earnings percentages.

Jam Sessions

One method for hooking up with musicians is to go to jam sessions. These gatherings provide an opportunity not only to meet other musicians but also to see how well you actually perform with others. When playing at jam sessions, it's best to avoid showboating. If you show off—in order to prove that you are the best drummer in the room—you will probably make the wrong impression. Instead, keep it straightforward and focus on the requirements of the music. This means playing like a team player. A jam session is a proving ground. However, quality musicians will be looking for taste, style, and appropriateness more than how many notes you can fit into a bar or how many different fills you can cram into a song. At jam sessions, remember stylistic concerns, too. For example, if you're playing a country rock ballad, you should not show off your double pedal skills or your Dave Weckl-inspired polyrhythms. The best drummers know when they're going overboard or playing something that just doesn't fit.

Cover Bands

Once you find players who have similar tastes and goals, work on developing a repertoire. You may want to write your own material or cowrite songs with others. You also might choose to play covers. Covers are interpretations of other people's music. There are two types of cover bands.

The first kind of cover band is called a tribute band. These groups focus on cover music by a single legendary band. For example, there are Rolling Stones tribute bands, Led Zeppelin tribute bands, and Pink Floyd tribute bands. However, most cover bands play a mixture of tunes by various artists. The average cover band plays an assortment of classic rock tunes with a few newer selections thrown in to stay current. For instance, cover bands might play a Journey single, a Steve Miller Band hit, a classic rocker by The Who, and then an Aerosmith ballad. They might also play a recent chart topper by Maroon 5 or John Mayer. With cover bands, the repertoire can really vary!

Realistic Expectations

Generally speaking, cover bands make more money than original groups, as they play private gatherings such as weddings, bar mitzvahs, holiday parties, and corporate events in additon to a variety of clubs and bars. Original rock bands inhabit the "rock" club scene, which is usually limited to a few local venues. At these venues, you may find yourself competing for stage time, since rock clubs tend to book several bands per night. Additonally, you may not make much money playing orignial music in clubs. The only exceptions to this are signed touring acts and extraordinary independent bands that have cultivated a large, dedicated following. Both situations are becoming increasingly rare.

In some cases, you may find that you actually lose money when you play clubs. Because of this, you should think about what your objectives are as a band. As you review your band goals, don't lose track of your personal aspirations; it's important to be mindful of your own needs, too. If your group is interested in music strictly as a hobby, then performing and recording will probably be a lot of fun. However, if you're looking to make a lot of money, sign with a major record label, tour the globe, ride in limos, and play *The Tonight Show*, you might be headed for disappointment. In truth, fame is rare. Thousands of bands exist; only a select few become rock stars, and often, sheer luck determines this.

When playing in any type of band, the best attitude to have is one of careful optimism. You should always work hard to make your dreams a reality. However, you must also accept the unpredictable nature of the performing arts. If things don't quite go as planned, you have to be able to brush it off, stay focused on the music, and move on.

Some gigs will be good; others will be a drag. Some shows will be profitable; you'll lose your shirt on others. Sometimes you'll have a large, attentive audience; other times, you'll have eight people talking over your set at the bar. However, if you can keep things in perspective—especially when things don't go as planned—you'll enjoy the experience of performing in a band a lot more.

Playing Other Styles of Music

Even though this book emphasizes rock and pop drumming, some mention should be made about other genres of music. Why? Because rock does not exist in a bubble. As mentioned in Chapter 1, rock is a collection and accumulation of many genres. Its antecedents are blues and country and western, and modern rock embraces elements from virtually every other major style of music. These styles include, but are not limited to, American folk, European classical, jazz, Latin, and other world music styles.

This is not to say that every artist culls from all of these styles. However, rock artists collectively have their hands dipped in just about every stylistic pot. For instance, The Beatles borrowed from Indian ragas. Sting dabbles in jazz. Paul Simon draws from South and West African music. David Byrne has experimented with Afro-Cuban music. Peter Gabriel features a wide variety of world music in his repertoire. Emerson, Lake & Palmer appropriated European classical, and The Pogues combined punk with traditional Celtic music. These disparate examples are but a drop in the bucket; the list could go on indefinitely.

FACT

Contemporary rock drummers must recognize the monumental influence of rap, hip-hop, and modern R&B in twenty-first-century rock and pop. These urban styles are very drum oriented. They also rule the airwaves and the charts. Consequently, you need to know how to play these genres or risk sounding old-fashioned and even passé.

In general, if you are going to get gigs, make yourself marketable, or even recruit other players to join your band, you should be aware of rock's complex relationships with dozens of other styles of music. Rock is truly multicultural and multilingual, and more and more, musicians are expected to understand other styles of music in order to play "x" rock hybrid; every decade brings with it new combinations and amalgamations. If you want to play drums in the rock band of the future, you're going to have to learn about several other major styles. You cannot learn about every genre; however, you should know something about jazz and Latin music.

Jazz and Latin are pat terms that apply to a whole array of substyles. To whittle it down: You should be able to play a good two-beat and four-beat swing beat with brushes and sticks. You should also be able to play a bossa nova and samba together with a wide variety of Afro-Cuban grooves. These include the merengue, cha-cha, rumba, mambo, and so on. Plus, you should learn how to play island styles such as the calypso, soca, reggae, and ska. You don't need to be an expert at all these styles; you just need to learn a few basic beats and variations so you can get by without stumbling and looking musically uninformed. All drummers should be able to play funky grooves, which can be applied to an assortment of urban and R&B styles. Since this is a cousin to rock, funk genres are detailed in Chapter 11.

Chapter 19

Equipment Guide

Purchasing the right equipment is very important. Having the most expensive or fancy gear is not. As you begin to define your goals and solidify your musical interests, you will be able to make better decisions about what drums, cymbals, hardware, sticks, pads, and other equipment you will want to use for practice and performance. You may even begin to think about what your dream set up might be. At this stage, however, it is important to make smart and reasonable purchases. This probably doesn't mean spending thousands of dollars on a vintage or top-of-the-line kit.

Choosing the Right Drum Set for You

There isn't only one kit that will work best for you. There are many great drum manufacturers and many great drum sets. Choosing Ludwig over Pearl, Yamaha over Gretsch, Slingerland over Tama, or Drum Workshop over Premier is a lot like choosing a McIntosh over a Granny Smith or a Red Delicious over a Golden Delicious. They may be different apples, but they are all pretty darn tasty.

You will read ads in drum magazines that include celebrity testimonials about X drum company. So-and-so "rock legend" will say that X brand is "the most resonant, perfectly crafted, blah, blah, blah drums in the world." In truth, all major drum manufacturers make high-quality instruments, and you will do well by any of these companies. See Appendix B for a list of trusted manufacturers and their websites.

ESSENTIAL

Climate control is essential to the health of your drum set. Extreme cold temperatures can cause shell veneers to peel off and/or crack. Consistent contact with moisture can also cause chrome on your rims and hardware to rust and tarnish. Even though you hit drums, they can be damaged easier than you think.

When choosing a drum kit, rather than focusing on brand names, think about price and desired use. Choose the highest-quality kit based on the amount of money you can or wish to spend. This may mean choosing a used kit. If so, don't be afraid of drums with a few nicks or scratches. As long as there are no cracks in the shells or warped hoops, used gear is perfectly acceptable. It can even be preferable.

Choosing the Right Shell Sizes

Choose your drum kit based on the type of music you will be playing. If you're playing loud rock, you'll want to purchase a kit that has at least a 22"-diameter kick drum. Ideally, you should use a drum with a good amount of depth. This will help you get a bigger, or fatter, tone. In this case, choose an 18" × 22" or 18" × 24" drum. Deeper tom-toms—often called power toms—are also recommended for loud rock playing. This means that, on a five-piece kit, your rack toms will be 10" × 12" and 11" × 13", respectively.

If you're playing hard rock or alternative rock, your snare drum could vary depending on personal taste. However, you probably would not want to use a piccolo snare (often 3.5" × 14" or 3" × 13"). These are better suited for funk or light jazz where a high-pitched crackle—without any bottom or low end—is desired. For hard rock, you'd likely choose a standard 5.5" × 14" snare; the shell could be made of wood or metal. Again, shell types come down to personal preference.

Some heavy hitters enjoy deeper snares so they can get a really fat sound. In this case, a 6.5" shell—or deeper—would be desirable. Snare drums can be as deep as 10"! A large-diameter floor tom would also be recommended. The standard size is 16" × 16".

ALERT!

If you plan to hit hard, purchase heavy-duty cymbal stands. This means buying stands that have double-braced legs and a strong wing-bolt system. Also, be sure to set up your cymbal stands so the legs form an even and stable tripod. The cymbal tilter must also be able to withstand a lot of force.

What if you're not playing ear-splitting rock? Maybe you just joined a folk-rock band or you plan to play in a soft-rock band down at the local bar and grill. In these cases, you won't need such a thunderous drum kit. Therefore, you might purchase a smaller bass drum (18" × 20"), one standard-size rack tom (8" × 12"), and a smaller floor tom (14" × 14"). Your hardware also does not need to be heavy duty. For example, you might choose single-braced cymbal stands, which are lighter and easier to cart around.

Ultimately, you need to get a sense of the music you will be playing and choose a kit based on how loud or soft you will be playing. To summarize, virtually every major drum manufacturer makes drums of varying depths and diameters, so don't limit yourself by considering only one company. Instead, keep an open mind and look for good deals.

What if I play a variety of musical styles?
If you plan to play in many different genres, choose drum sizes from the middle of the size spectrum. You might choose a 16″ × 22″ kick and standard-size snare and tom-toms. If anything, bigger is better than smaller. Tiny cocktail kits or other small portable sets have little use in rock music.

If you're a beginner, it's okay to buy student-model kits. Most entry-level kits made by major manufacturers are quite functional. For example, the Ludwig Accent CS Combo is playable. Yamaha's Rydeen model is very good, and Tama's Imperialstar is the best of the lot. However, you will likely need to replace the heads on all student-model kits; the skins that come on these sets are almost always cheap and dent easily.

When replacing heads, buy only Evans, Remo, or Aquarian brands. Single-ply batter heads are best on the snare drum. For the bass drum, you should use a heavier double-ply head. You may use either single- or double-ply heads on the tom-toms. If you want more attack and articulation, you should try single-ply heads. On the downside, you will get more overtones and more ring with single-ply heads because they are thinner. If you want a rounder, studio-produced sound, you should use double-ply heads. However, these thicker heads get less attack and less colorful overtones

You will also want to avoid using the cymbals that come with student-model kits. These are usually poorly made, and dreadful cymbals will only make you sound dreadful. This goes for hi-hat cymbals, too; lousy hi-hats get an especially weak chick sound.

Buying Cymbals

The big-three cymbal manufacturers are Zildjian, Sabian, and Paiste. Zildjian is recognized as the oldest company in the world, dating back to the 1600s. They also far outsell any other cymbal manufacturer. However, this doesn't mean that Zildjian is the only quality cymbal company or even the best. Sabian and Paiste make fantastic products, and all three companies offer a wide variety of cymbals, hi-hats, and novelty items.

Other lesser-known companies such as Istanbul (Agop and Mehmet), Bosphorus, and Meinl also make world-class cymbals. Istanbul and Bosphorus offer genuine hand-hammered cymbals made exclusively in Turkey. Meinl offers a hand-hammered Turkish line of cymbals too, although most of their models are manufactured in Germany. Wuhan is another superb cymbal manufacturer from China, and they use cymbal-making techniques dating back two millennia. UfiP, from Italy, are also highly regarded. Their slogan is "ear-created cymbals," and they are gradually becoming more popular internationally.

Bosphorus is a relatively new cymbal company, but their cymbal manufacturing techniques date back centuries. Their motto is "one man, one hammer, one cymbal." Without a doubt, their product line is as good as the big-three companies, if not superior. For the rock player, their Gold-model cymbals offer warmth, projection, and durability. They are also 100 percent hand hammered. Many argue that hand hammering, as opposed to machine hammering, brings out the rich timbral nuances in cymbals.

ESSENTIAL

The biggest problem with cymbals is their cost. Professional ride cymbals range from $200–$1,000. Given such a span, used cymbals may be your best bet. In fact, shiny cymbals fresh from the plant sometimes lack the depth, expression, and tonal complexity found in preowned cymbals.

Student-model cymbals are okay if you plan to play only in your home or with friends in the garage. However, if you have plans to play in public, you should only use pro-model cymbals. Can't afford them? Again, buy used cymbals. Zildjian are a good place to start. They are not overly pricey (even when new) and they are quite versatile. On the downside, there are many superior models available by Zildjian and their competitors. For example, Zildjian's K series is a classic. Paiste's Signature series and Sabian's AA and

Signature series are also excellent. If you do choose entry-level cymbals, Zildjian's ZBT and ZXT series are functional. They also come in boxed sets for ease in purchasing.

Drumsticks

There are many stick companies and models available to you. Many drummers contend that Vic Firth's pitch-matched sticks help drummers create a more consistent sound. However, the finish and lacquer used on Regal Tip sticks allows you to maintain a very relaxed grip. Regal Tip calls their product a "superior gripping stick."

Other prominent companies include Promark, Zildjian, and Vater. For beginners, it is important to use a medium-sized stick such as the Vic Firth American Classic or the Regal Tip 5A. As stated in Chapter 5, you may want to use a meatier stick for loud rock. For this, a 5B model may be best. Regarding length, choose a stick that is around 16" long. No matter what stick you choose, it should be versatile. Therefore, overly fat or gigantic "tree trunks" are not recommended. Also, buy only hickory or oak sticks; stay away from maple sticks, as they are soft and will dent and splinter easily.

The standard tip, or bead, on the end of a stick is wooden. However, nylon tips are popular with many of today's drummers. The only real difference between wooden and nylon tips is that the latter has a brighter, more distinct tone on cymbals. For this reason, nylon tips work well in loud musical settings. Nylon tips are also more durable; wooden tips can chip over time. However, some drummers have had problems with nylon tips ungluing and falling off.

ESSENTIAL

Before purchasing a pair of sticks, hold each stick loosely, tap them together, and listen to the sound. A good pair of sticks should have the same pitch. They should also be the same weight. Properly paired sticks allow you to play your best. Not only are they more comfortable in your hands, you will get a more consistent, even tone.

Regardless of the brand, model, or tip, don't let anyone sell you metal or plastic sticks. Stick shafts should always be wooden; metal and plastic sticks are novelty items and will only interfere with your ability to develop proper technique. Furthermore, discounted sticks (you may see them lying around in boxes at stores) are almost always defective and should be avoided.

Before purchasing a pair of sticks, make sure you first roll each stick on a flat surface. If the stick wobbles, that means the stick is warped. Don't buy it! Misshapen sticks have an inconsistent tone. They also feel awkward in your hands and your performance will be compromised.

Brushes, Rods, and Mallets

Beginners needn't worry about purchasing brushes right away, but if you're a performing drummer, you should own them and try to find uses for them. Brush playing is a lost art; why not find creative ways to bring it back to life?

You never know when a performance opportunity will arise when brushes can be used. Brushes are used in jazz a lot. They are sometimes used in country and western music, too. However, rock drummers don't use them enough. Why not try them out on a soft introduction or in the studio as an overdubbed drum track? Come up with your own uses and add color and spice to your playing and your band's songs.

QUESTIONS

What are brushes?
They are metallic or nylon bristles that attach to a metal, wooden, or rubber-coated shaft. The bristles fan out from the shaft and are raked across the drumhead or cymbal to create a subtle "white noise" effect. Say, "Shhhhhh" aloud. The sound of your voice is not unlike the sound of a brush being combed across a snare-drum head.

Like drumsticks, brushes come in a variety of shapes and sizes and several different companies manufacture them. It's difficult to say which type or brand is best for you, although the Regal Tip 550W and 583R are both beautiful sounding on drums and cymbals. They also feel very comfortable in the hands. If you do buy brushes, make sure to buy the retractable kind—the brushes can be drawn back into the shaft. Usually, brush companies refer to this as telescoping brushes. Nonretractable brushes have a shorter lifespan, since the exposed bristles often become tangled and bent like used paintbrushes.

A cousin to the brush is a specialty stick featuring thick wooden or thermoplastic dowels. These dowels are banded together with plastic strips. Many stick companies make this type of accessory, and generically they are called rods. Specifically, Vic Firth calls their product a Rute, and Promark calls theirs, alternately, a Hot Rod or Lightning Rod. Both are made of several wooden dowels bound together. Regal Tip's product, the Blastick, is a little different because it contains plastic bristles. Rods may be used when a jazz brush is too light but a solid drumstick is too heavy. Often, you'll see rock drummers using rods in unplugged or quieter situations.

As you might have guessed, mallets also come in many shapes and sizes and many companies make them. As a rock drummer, you will have limited use for them, but it's always good to keep a pair in your stick bag. In rock, mallets are used mostly for big cymbal rolls or timpani-like tom-tom parts. Often, these parts are grandiose in nature.

What is a mallet? A mallet is a stick with a soft, rounded felt head. As a drum set player, you will only use tympani mallets on your drums and cymbals. Vic Firth and Musser (Ludwig) both make quality mallets. Vic Firth's T1 General is very good, as is the Musser Payson Model Medium Mallet (L-306). You don't need to buy expensive, imported, or hand-made mallets; just about any name-brand semi-soft felt mallet should meet your needs.

Drum Pads and Music Stands

Drum pads are an essential part of every drummer's collection. Beginners often can't afford drums themselves, so pads take on even more relevancy. One of the best pads on the market is the gum-rubber RealFeel pad made by HQ Percussion. They have a couple of different options. First, they offer a single-sided pad with a gum-rubber playing surface. Second, they offer a double-sided pad comprised of gum rubber and neoprene, respectively. These pads come in two sizes: a smaller 6" pad and a larger 12" pad. You may also purchase a stand for the smaller pad or use a snare drum stand to hold the larger one. Promark's XPAD, made from a blue rubber compound, is comparable to HQ's RealFeel, as is Vic Firth's VICPAD 9 and 12. All of these pads will give you the necessary bounce you need to develop good technique.

The Remo Drum Company makes fine pads and drum pad sets too, though they are louder than the above-mentioned pads. This is because their pads use real Coated Ambassador drumheads. On the upside, these heads can be tuned—to a certain extent—by using a screwdriver, and the feel is very close to a snare drum.

Since drums themselves can be very loud, practice pads offer a wonderful alternative to supplying earplugs for your entire neighborhood. Do yourself a favor and make a pad and or pad set one of your first purchases. Keep in mind that if you cannot afford an actual drum set, pads are a legitimate alternative. In other words, you can develop nearly all the necessary techniques and skills needed to be a drummer with only pads; every serious drummer works out on pads at least part of the time.

If you prefer to play on your actual drums but the racket is waking up the neighbors, try using drum set mutes, or silencers. Both HQ Percussion and Vic Firth make pads that sit on top of your actual drums. Zildjian also makes silencers for cymbals. Never use noise ordinances as an excuse for not practicing again.

Not much needs to be said about music stands, except to buy one. You do not need a fancy or expensive stand. A simple fold-up wire stand will do. Too often, students place their music on a chair or a desk, only to crane their neck around to read the notes. If you do this, you'll run the risk of developing bad posture and technique. Don't place your method books on an unused tom-tom either. The vibrations of the drums will only cause them to fall to the ground over and over. How frustrating is that? Buy yourself a stand and be comfortable while you practice.

Appendix A

Essential Recordings, Books, and Films/DVDs

This appendix lists the essentials for any student of rock and fusion drumming. However, this list is by no means exhaustive. There are many artists not listed here who have contributed something significant to the great conversation of rock and pop music. Note: Not every historically important album by the artists listed here appears in this appendix. Therefore, use this list only as a credible point of departure.

Essential Recordings

The following recordings are listed as: **Artist—** *Album(s)* (Drummer)

AC/DC—ial*Back in Black* (Phil Rudd)

The Beach Boys—*Pet Sounds* (Hal Blaine)

The Beatles—*Meet the Beatles, Sgt. Pepper's Lonely Hearts Club Band, The White Album, Abbey Road* (Ringo Starr)

Black Sabbath—*Paranoid* (Bill Ward)

James Brown—*In the Jungle Groove* (Various)

The Clash—*London Calling* (Topper Headon)

Cream—*Disraeli Gears* and *Wheels of Fire* (Ginger Baker)

Deep Purple—*Machine Head* and *Deep Purple in Rock* (Ian Paice)

The Doors—*The Doors, Strange Days, Waiting for the Sun* (John Densmore)

Emerson, Lake & Palmer—*Emerson, Lake & Palmer* and *Tarkus* (Carl Palmer)

Focus—*Moving Waves* (Pierre van der Linden)

Peter Gabriel—*So* and *Secret World Live* (Manu Katché)

Genesis—*Selling England By the Pound* and *A Trick of the Tail* (Phil Collins)

Buddy Holly—*The "Chirping" Crickets* and *Buddy Holly* (Jerry Allison)

Iron Maiden—*Killers* (Clive Burr) and *Piece of Mind* (Nicko McBrain)

Jimi Hendrix Experience—*Are You Experienced, Axis: Bold as Love, Electric Ladyland* (Mitch Mitchell)

Journey—*Escape* and *Frontiers* (Steve Smith)

Judas Priest—*Stained Class* (Les Binks)

King Crimson—*Red* and *Three of a Perfect Pair* (Bill Bruford)

The Kinks—*You Really Got Me* and *The Kinks Are the Village Green Preservation Society* (Mick Avory)

KISS—*Alive!* (Peter Criss)

Led Zeppelin—*Led Zeppelin I, II, III,* and *Houses of the Holy* (John Bonham)

Mahavishnu Orchestra—*The Inner Mounting Flame, Birds of Fire, The Lost Trident Sessions* (Billy Cobham)

Metallica—*Master of Puppets* and *St. Anger* (Lars Ulrich)

Nirvana—*Nevermind* (Dave Grohl)

Parliament—*Up for the Down Stroke* and *Mothership Connection* (Various)

The Police—*Regatta De Blanc, Ghost in the Machine, Synchronicity* (Stewart Copeland)

Elvis Presley—*Elvis Presley* (D. J. Fontana)

The Ramones—*Ramones* and *Rocket to Russia* (Tommy Ramone)

The Rolling Stones—*Aftermath, Beggars Banquet, Some Girls, Tattoo You* (Charlie Watts)

Rush—*Permanent Waves, Exit...Stage Left, Roll the Bones, Snakes and Arrows* (Neil Peart)

Bruce Springsteen—*Born to Run* (Max Weinberg)

Steely Dan—*Aja* (Various)

Sting—*Dream of the Blue Turtles* (Omar Hakim) and *Ten Summoner's Tales* (Vinnie Colaiuta)

U2—*Joshua Tree* and *How to Dismantle an Atomic Bomb* (Larry Mullen Jr.)

Van Halen—*1984* (Alex Van Halen)

Vanilla Fudge—*Vanilla Fudge* and *The Beat Goes On* (Carmine Appice)

Dave Weckl—*Rhythm of the Soul* and *Perpetual Motion* (Dave Weckl)

The Who—*The Who Sings My Generation, Tommy, Who's Next* (Keith Moon)

Tony Williams—*Life Time* and *Emergency!* (Tony Williams)

Yes—*Fragile* (Bill Bruford)

Frank Zappa—*Joe's Garage* (Vinnie Colaiuta) and *Baby Snakes* (Terry Bozzio)

Essential Instructional Books

Snare Drum/Technique

Black, Dave and Sandy Feldstein. *Alfred's Drums Method, Book I.* (Alfred Publishing, 2006)

Morello, Joe. *Master Studies.* (Hal Leonard, 1989)

Morello, Joe. *Master Studies II: More Exercises for the Development and Control and Technique.* (Modern Drummer Publications, 2006)

Reed, Ted. *Progressive Steps to Syncopation for the Modern Drummer.* (Alfred Publishing, 1997)

Stone, George Lawrence. *Accents and Rebounds for the Snare Drummer.* (George B. Stone & Son, Inc. 1961)

Stone, George Lawrence. *Stick Control for the Snare Drummer.* (George B. Stone & Son, Inc., 1998)

Wilcoxon, Charley. *Modern Rudimental Swing Solos for the Advanced Drummer.* (Ludwig Publishing, 1979)

Drum Set

Appice, Carmine. *The Ultimate Realistic Rock Drum Method.* (Warner Brothers, 2000)

Bailey, Colin. *Bass Drum Control.* (Hal Leonard, 1998)

Briggs, Frank. *Mel Bay's Complete Modern Drumset.* (Mel Bay Publications, 1994)

Bruford, Bill. *When in Doubt, Roll!* (Modern Drummer Publications, 1988)

Dahlgreen, Marvin and Elliot Fin. *4-Way Coordination: A Method Book for the Development of Complete Independence on the Drum Set.* (Alfred Publishing, 1999)

Franco, Joe. *Double Bass Drumming.* (Warner Brothers, 1993)

Pickering, John and Frank Briggs. *Mel Bay The Drummer's Cookbook.* (Mel Bay Publications Inc., 2005)

Other

Starr, Eric. *The Everything Drums Book: From Tuning and Timing to Fills and Solos—All You Need to Keep the Beat.* (Adams Media, 2003)

Essential Films and Instructional DVDs

Appice, Carmine. *The Ultimate Realistic Rock Drum Method.* (Alfred Publishing, 2007)

Baker, Ginger. *Master Drum Technique.* (Hot Licks, 2006)

The Beatles. *Let it Be.* (Audiotape, Inc., 1970)

Blackman, Cindy. *Multiplicity: Cindy Blackman's Drum World.* (Hal Leonard, 1998)

Led Zeppelin. *The Song Remains the Same.* (Warner Home Studio, 1999)

Metallica. *Metallica: Some Kind of Monster.* (Paramount, 2005)

Morello, Joe. *Drum Method 1: The Natural Approach to Technique.* (Hot Licks/Music Sales Corp., 2006)

Peart, Neil. *A Work In Progress.* (Warner Brothers Publications, 2002)

Peart, Neil. *Anatomy of a Drum Solo.* (Hudson Music / Rounder Records, 2005)

The Police. *Synchronicity Concert.* (A&M, 2005)

Various Artists. *Classic Drum Solos and Drum Battles.* (Hal Leonard, 2001)

Various Artists. *Classic Jazz Drummers: Swing and Beyond.* (Hudson Music, 2002)

Weckl, Dave. *How to Develop Technique.* (New York DVD, 2003)

Appendix B

Essential Websites

Recognizing that most people get their information from online sources, it seems only fitting to include an essential websites appendix. Below is a list of respectable websites that will help you learn more about rock drumming as discussed in this book.

This list focuses mostly on manufacturers' websites, though some educational sites are also provided. Over time, it's likely this information will change. Therefore, you still need to conduct your own smart Internet research. Tip: If you want to look up information on artists, it's best to trust official websites. Beware of well-intentioned but sometimes inaccurate fan sites.

Drums Sets
Most Famous Manufacturers

www.ludwig-drums.com
www.yamahadrums.com
www.pearldrum.com
www.tama.com
www.gretschdrums.com
www.gibson.com/en-us/Divisions/Slingerland
www.dwdrums.com
www.premier-percussion.com

www.mapexdrums.com
www.sonor.com

Other Quality Drum Manufacturers

www.ayottedrums.com
www.tayedrums.com
www.noblecooley.com
www.gmsdrums.com
www.bradydrums.com.au
www.groovepercussion.com (Specializes in student-model kits)

Drumheads

www.remo.com (Also drum sets and pads)
www.evansdrumheads.com (Inventors of the plastic head)
www.aquariandrumheads.com

Cymbals
Most Famous

www.zildjian.com (Also makes sticks)
www.paiste.com
www.sabian.com

Other Quality Manufacturers

www.bosphoruscymbals.com
www.istanbulcymbals.com
www.istanbulmehmet.com
www.meinlcymbals.com
www.ufip.com
www.wuhancymbals.com

Drumsticks

www.promark-stix.com
www.vicfirth.com
www.regaltip.com
www.vater.com
www.hotsticksdrumsticks.com

Miscellaneous Equipment

www.hqpercussion.com (drum pads)
www.groverpro.com (snare drums, percussion instruments, sticks, and mallets)
www.lpmusic.com (Latin percussion instruments)
www.rhythmtech.com (tambourines and other percussion instruments)

Educational Links

www.drums.com
www.drumming.com
www.drum-talk.com
www.drums-and-drum sets.com
www.drumbum.com
www.howtoplaydrums.com
www.drummerworld.com (Lots of free videos and MP3s of drummers performing)
www.intellectualmusician.com
www.wikipedia.org

Other Important Sites

www.pas.org (Percussive Arts Society)
www.pasic.org (Annual Drum and Percussion Convention)
www.moderndrummer.com (Most popular drumming magazine in the world)
www.drummagazine.com (Another popular magazine specializing in rock)
www.amazon.com (Most essential recordings, method books, and instructional DVDs can be purchased here)

Index